D1561092

CENSORSHIP
OF EXPRESSION
IN THE 1980s

Recent Titles in
Contributions to the Study of Mass Media and Communications

CENSORSHIP OF EXPRESSION IN THE 1980s

A Statistical Survey

John B. Harer
and
Steven R. Harris

Contributions to the Study of Mass Media and Communications,
Number 45

GREENWOOD PRESS
Westport, Connecticut • London

Library of Congress Cataloging-in-Publication Data

Harer, John B.
    Censorship of expression in the 1980s : a statistical survey /
John B. Harer and Steven R. Harris.
        p. cm. — (Contributions to the study of mass media and
communications, ISSN 0732–4456 ; no. 45.)
    Includes bibliographical references (p.) and index.
    ISBN 0–313–28746–5 (alk. paper)
    1. Censorship—United States—Statistics. I. Harris, Steven R.
(Steven Robert) II. Title. III. Series.
Z658.U5H37 1994
323.44′0973′021—dc20   94–875

British Library Cataloguing in Publication Data is available.

Library of Congress Catalog Card Number: 94–875
ISBN: 0–313–28746–5
ISSN: 0732–4456

First published in 1994

Greenwood Press, 88 Post Road West, Westport, CT 06881
An imprint of Greenwood Publishing Group, Inc.

Printed in the United States of America

The paper used in this book complies with the
Permanent Paper Standard issued by the National
Information Standards Organization (Z39.48–1984).

10 9 8 7 6 5 4 3 2 1

Copyright Acknowledgments

Tables 4.3 and 4.4 and Figures 4.2(a-d), 4.3(a-d), 4.4(a-d), and 4.5(a-d) have been reprinted from the
Newsletter on Intellectual Freedom by permission of the American Library Association.

To those colleagues and mentors who have influenced me the most as a librarian and civil libertarian, especially:

Jim Percey, Bloomsburg University of Pennsylvania
Dr. Bernard Vavrek, Clarion University of Pennsylvania
The members of the North Central Chapter of the American
  Civil Liberties Union of Pennsylvania, especially Martha Donohue
Isabel Berney, Pulaski County (Virginia) Schools
Allen Bonney Brooks, Virginia Library Association
Anne Briggs, Maryland Library Association
Jeanette McVeigh, Towson State University

John B. Harer

To my mother, Annette Harris.

Steven R. Harris

Contents

Tables and Figures

TABLES

FIGURES

Preface

The United States of America has grown to be the most powerful and influential nation in the world in just two hundred years. Many scholars have attributed this to our unique form of democratic government. As early as 1835, for example, Alexis de Tocqueville heralded the greatness of "democracy in America." However, it is clear from a study of constitutional history that this country's prominence in the world could not have occurred without the protection of free expression as guaranteed by the First Amendment. It is doubtful that our nation would exist as we know it without passage of this amendment, for many of our founding fathers believed that without individual liberties, the rights of human-kind and the principles of self-governance for which the Revolution was fought,that struggle would have been for nought. Many nations of the world have modeled most or part of the U.S. Constitution in their system of govern-ment. However, no nation has risen to the level of freedom our people enjoy because the vision of the great men of the Revolution for a more perfect government provided us with the Bill of Rights, which establishes a broader set of individual liberties than any other political system and protects those rights with a system of checks and balances on the three branches of government. As the first and most important of the amendments that are the Bill of Rights, the First Amendment to the U.S. Constitution guarantees four expressive rights to all citizens: freedom of religion, speech, the press, and the right to assemble peacefully. The volumes of publications on the subject of the First Amendment and free expression are numerous and have been the subject of much scholarly work. However, the lofty ideals and principles of the scholars are not always understood or accepted by the average citizen. The manner in which the people exercise these rights is a common every day experience that can tend to obscure the more philosophical aspects for many individuals. Free speech activities are so much a part of the lives of all people that this freedom is often taken for granted. Only when a challenge or complaint about an expressive act is made is there possibly any realization that such rights are to be protected, if at all.

Expression in its many forms--books, film, plays, art, speech and so forth-- occurs far more often than an act of censorship. In the scheme of things, censorship may not appear to be a substantive evil if viewed only as a portion of the total amount of expressive activity. However, this is because the number of known censorship incidents is dwarfed by the tremendous amount of expression in its various forms. The very success of our freedoms in promoting expression, then, threatens their existence as some societal forces seek to use censorship to close off some of those activities to further their own goals. The politically motivated limitations on liberty place our democratic ideals into jeopardy.

It is for these reasons that intellectual freedom as a phenomena must be held in the forefront of our national consciousness. If there are legitimate limitations to expression, then each should be carefully weighed and pass time-honored tests within society's framework for expression interaction. The pressure for censorship on a personal level is too often driven by the emotional moment. Any understanding of what free expression for anyone can be must be grounded first in the heritage and legacy of the American Revolution and the ratification of the constitution adopted in 1787. This has been the purview of the scholarly world for years, but this understanding also requires a knowledge of how these lofty principles play themselves out in the real world. A study of censorship incidents becomes so crucial because of this latter argument. Knowledge of what expressive activities cause difficulties and why they are so troublesome enriches our ability as a nation to make a fair and just application of those freedoms that have made this country so strong and unique.

This publication is intended to increase our understanding of censorship and why it occurs. It is a statistical survey of reported incidents during the decade 1981 - 1990. Empirical data are sometimes viewed as dull or passionless. That is not necessarily true of statistics on censorship. First, nothing about censorship can ever be passionless. It is a naturally polarizing topic. The information found in this text has been rendered as objectively as possible. Objectivity, however, should not be construed as a failure to take a stand on the issue. It is the first and most important requirement of any reasoned viewpoint, but we are committed to preserving intellectual freedom and to keeping the boundaries of free expression as broad as possible. A legitimate research design has been used to gather and compile the data, which is explained in Chapter 3. The data has been presented in a straightforward manner for use by any person or group who may have a need for such statistics. We have endeavored to explain the data as objectively as possible, but it is our profound hope that this work will contribute to a greater understanding of censorship in order to reduce its negative effects on expressive activity.

This book contains six chapters and an appendix. The first three chapters are designed to provide a background explanation of the topic and a description of the methodology used to conduct the study. Chapter 1 is an overview of intellectual freedom principles and the state of intellectual freedom during the 1980s. Chapters 2 and 3 follow a design suitable for similar research. The literature review of Chapter 2 focuses on publications on censorship that are also research oriented. The methodology utilized is explained in Chapter 3.

The final three chapters report the results of our research. This is accomplished in three forms. Chapter 4 lists and explains the data as compiled under the guidelines of the methodology. An analysis of each aspect found in the data is included. Using the ten attributes of a censorship incident detailed in the methodology chapter, a total picture of what occurred during the Reagan era (1981-1990) can be understood. Second, a comparison of the data from this decade with quantitative research from past decades is included in Chapter 5. This comparison provides a means for benchmarking the results for evaluating them beyond a straightforward listing of statistics. A comparison of the sources used to collect the data is also included, and a review of each source evaluates their effectiveness for reporting censorship information. As this evaluation has noted, the most significant source used for this research has been *The Newsletter on Intellectual Freedom*. It is published six times per year by the American Library Association's Office for Intellectual Freedom. The last chapter synthesizes the results to provide a general conclusion of what the state of expressive activity has been during the 1980s and answers ten research questions posed in the research design. There is an extensive list of all items for which a censorship attempt has been recorded by the reporting sources in the appendix.

This research has compiled a substantial amount of data on censored materials in all forms of expression. No attempt has been made to analyze all aspects of the data, however. Ten research questions are postulated and the goal of answering these questions is met, and an analysis is performed on other facets found in the data. The focus has been primarily on general forms of expression. One of the reporting sources is devoted exclusively to student journalism. A basic coverage of the information from this source has been performed, but a more in depth analysis has been set aside for future efforts.

Our freedoms are a precious commodity. To protect them requires vigilance on the part of all citizens, but falls more heavily on the shoulders of those whose profession is entrusted with some aspect of creating, interpreting, or preserving an expressive form. Such a definition touches millions of Americans. We hope that this book, at least in some small way, will be a resource for those concerned with our basic liberties.

Acknowledgments

Any project the size of this publication cannot be undertaken without the help and advice of many other individuals, and this book is no exception. We would like to take this opportunity to thank some very special people. First, and most important, our heartfelt gratitude is due to Janell Passick. She has been a tireless assistant whose support has only been surpassed by her excellent technical expertise and advice. She is truly a very gifted individual whose talent produced many of the tables and graphs. By the same token, we also must thank our two other production assistants, Julie Raymond and Kelly Reoh, for their time and the hard work they gave us. They helped produce large sections of the copy, for which we are eternally grateful.

As this research began, we needed advice on the best data program to compile the statistics. Mel Dodd, currently acting head of personnel for the Sterling C. Evans Library at Texas A&M University, was the most obvious choice for this counsel. We have always had the utmost respect for his seasoned and reasonable opinions, not to mention his good humor. His suggestion on which program was most efficient saved a great deal of time and trouble. Also, in this regard, OK Okonkwo lent his invaluable assistance and expertise on numerous occasions. Without his help, the production of the tables and graphs would have been more difficult.

Greenwood Press also must be commended for its willingness to publish the book. We are most grateful to Lynn Taylor for her encouragement in the initial stages of the publication and to our editors, James Dunton, James Ice, and especially Jude Grant for working with us on the production of the final copy. During the conduct of this research, we received substantial support from two university committees, the Texas A&M University Mini-Grant Committee and the Sterling C. Evans Library's Research Committee. Their generosity was most appreciated. We also wish to thank the administration of the Evans Library, especially Colleen Cook, Assistant Director for Technical Services and Collection Development, and Julia Rholes, Acting Assistant Director for Public

Services, for their support and understanding while we carried out our research and wrote the book. Their moral support and encouragement was invaluable. We are also beholden to the staff of the Evans Library's Access Services units, but most especially to Sandra Cooper, Tommy Schaffer, Susan Raschke, and OK Okonkwo, whose patience we tested more than once and who consistently demonstrated their loyalty and support under some very difficult conditions.

We would also like to thank four of the most influential intellectual freedom advocacy organizations in the country, i.e., People for the American Way, the Student Press Law Center, the National Coalition Against Censorship, and the American Library Association's Office for Intellectual Freedom, for allowing us to acquire and use their journals and newsletters for this research. However, a special thanks is due Marc Rosenblum of the National Coalition Against Censorship for his encouragement and support, and, as always, much is owed Judith Krug of the American Library Association's OIF, whose wealth of knowledge and depth of advice we have admired for many years and whose support has always been beyond reproach.

Last, we would be remiss if we failed to thank our families for their patience and understanding. A very special thanks goes out to Susan Meisel-Harer from John B. Harer for her courage and moral support in the production of this book.

1 Introduction

The election of Ronald Reagan in 1980 shocked and dismayed many civil libertarians and advocates of intellectual freedom. His conservative background was not the only cause for concern. His record as governor of California as well as many public pronouncements showed him to be openly hostile to civil liberties. But his election also appeared to embolden right-wing organizations, especially fundamentalist Christians just entering the political arena, such as the Moral Majority.

Even before Reagan took office, two members of the Moral Majority in Abingdon, Virginia, a minister and a county commissioner, began a vicious campaign against the Abingdon Public Library and its director, Kathy Williams, over books authored by Harold Robbins and Sidney Sheldon. The controversy exploded all over the national press and lasted almost a year. News analysis at the time focused on the connection between Reagan's election and the events that unfolded in Abingdon and predicted similar problems throughout the nation.

The Abingdon challenges were the opening salvos in a war between the left and right for a very difficult twelve- year period. During the late 1960s and early 1970s, the United States had a very conservative president as well, but the political climate was trending liberal. The anti-war movement fostered other liberal causes, such as the feminist and ecology movements, for example. It was during this era that L. B. Woods conducted, then published, a study of censorship challenges entitled *A Decade of Censorship in America*. If an era of liberal causes could ostensibly produce "a decade of censorship," it seemed reasonable to assume that a more conservative era would produce at least as much, if not more so, in the number and types of challenges since censorship is more often attributed to the right wing. This, then, became a primary motivating factor for producing this study.

The study of censorship is important for Americans, but not because we should be or can be shocked by the contents of a book, nor because a complaint about a seemingly innocuous creative work offends our sensibilities. Instead, censorship as a phenomena should be explored because it is a conflict between powerful opposing forces in society that can threaten its very foundation and ideals. It is a conflict because reasonable individuals in our society disagree as to what defines the limitations of creativity and expression and who should decide what has passed beyond the limits.

It is a dangerous conflict because the arguments used by opposing forces during censorship conflicts are played out in the political arena both locally and nationally by organizations and groups that possess real power. It is this power struggle that has the potential for reordering our democratic and constitutional principles, especially if a monopoly of power is secured by one of these forces or the struggle is won in the political arena by those who wish to restrict the Bill of Rights. Berns (1979) reported that a 1972 poll showed that two thirds of the respondents would not permit free speech to those who promote communism or atheist causes, for example. Given such facts, can we be sure that the First Amendment would continue to exist if a new constitutional convention were to be called and then controlled by the likes of the Moral Majority? It is highly doubtful.

It can easily be argued that a parent who files one formal complaint with a library about the access to one book will not destroy our democratic republic as we know it. It might even be said that a total accumulation of such events is not a serious threat to the nation's moral and intellectual fiber. The fact of the matter is that censorship of many books and other creative works has happened for years and our democratic ideals are still respected and revered by significant portions of the populace as well as notable national institutions. Intellectual freedom is enjoyed in the United States in a more unfettered manner than in any other nation on earth. In most third world nations, for instance, the press is strictly controlled or state owned and manipulated. In many industrialized nations, political expression is proscribed in some manner. Germans cannot form a Nazi party. The British cannot speak ill of the queen, for example.

However, the real problem lies within the question of what constitutes intellectual freedom as embodied in the First Amendment and constitutional law, both statutory and case law. A censorship incident is not only a struggle in a community for the rights and privileges of access to a created work, but also a struggle to determine if a society's desire for law and order, as often manifested in the cry for parental rights, outweighs individual liberties, especially freedom of speech and of the press. This conflict attracts powerful interests seeking to gain influence and control by taking sides and gaining mass support. Because these groups acquire power, they have the potential for redefining what constitutes the line between society's needs and individual rights. Such groups can elect politicians who will introduce legislation to restrict or change what can be said or created, lobby to influence the passage of such laws, and work for the appointment of judges who could interpret such laws or write court opinions affecting changes, in our liberties, with or without similar legislation often as a result of one local controversy. In recent years, this country has witnessed just such a scenario in the national debates over abortion laws and over hate-speech legislation. For example, after the Supreme Court legalized abortion, the debate in the political arena moved to the passage of the Hyde Amendment, written and supported by anti-abortion congressmen and their supporters, to limit funding of abortion services by the Federal Government. By the 1980s, we witnessed the election of two Republican presidents who packed the Supreme Court with conservative justices that restricted abortion rights as a result of power and influence gained by these powerful conservative groups. In one case, decided by this majority, *Rust v. Sullivan*, the Court upheld President Bush's gag order for health clinics receiving federal money on the grounds that abortion information can be withheld if the government so desires when the government sponsors such services. This came about over a dispute involving a New York health clinic that was receiving federal support. In this manner, one powerful conservative movement caused a drastic limitation in the dissemination of information and threatened the concept of absolute privilege enjoyed by medical professionals in order to further their national aims for restricted abortions.

The framework of the debate over censorship in the past three decades appears to be operating on two nonintersecting plains. The forces for intellectual freedom abhor censorship on the grounds that high democratic ideals must be protected. They favor an open society where free will gives each person the right to choose "truth" for themselves and where liberal, democratic axioms are promulgated to protect citizens from tyranny and repression. They often view individuals and groups who challenge materials as repressive censors or worse, "book burners." In *The Flight from Reason*, David Berninghausen argues, "Although intellectual freedom will be unpopular with extremists at both ends of the socio-political continuum, it is essential for the future of man, for if it is lost, the status quo, with all its inadequacies and injustices, will be most difficult to correct. Change is inevitable, but unless man uses his reason to weigh the alternatives, he has no grounds for even hoping that the change will be for the better. Without intellectual freedom and the opportunities afforded by the free, objective scholarship, man's illusions and misperceptions will go uncorrected or probably even increase, and our capacity to perceive and deal with our environment will be lost" (1975, 88).

In this defense of intellectual freedom, Berninghausen as well as others argue that intellectual freedom is an ideal that must be sought after and protected in its purest form as much as possible. This ideal is often defined by one of several philosophical discourses, such as John Milton's marketplace of ideas or John Stuart Mill's theory of social exchange. The anti-censorship forces battle restrictions on books and other works because it impedes the ability to reach this goal. If censorship of any item were to succeed, then people could not partake of Milton's marketplace freely because the work would not be available for individuals to choose it as the truth or not to choose it based on their own needs and biases, nor Mill's social exchange because the work would not be available to be traded as a false idea for a true one. These approaches revere the struggle for the ideal and combat any erosion in the state of free expression. For instance, Eli Oboler states, "To escape the restrictive bonds of government and society and the all-too-human limitations of individual prejudice and intolerance in regard to thought and its expression is a goal set by idealists throughout civilized history. Whether complete intellectual freedom for everyone is a reasonable aim or simply a chimera--an idealistic will-of-the-wisp that will help in the achievement of the lesser, but more attainable goals--is hardly worth arguing; the very act of working toward absolute individual freedom is a highly motivated, assuredly widely accepted activity which merits even wider support" (1980, 6).

In addition to striving for an ideal state of liberty, intellectual freedom is defended on the tenets of democracy and self-governance and the meaning of the First Amendment. Although these arguments are influenced and even framed in theories of free speech, the emphasis is on the importance of our constitutional principles. One of the greatest scholars of intellectual freedom, Alexander Meiklejohn wrote, "No one who reads with care the text of the First Amendment can fail to be startled by its absoluteness. The phrase, 'Congress shall make no law...abridging the freedom of speech,' is unqualified. It admits no exceptions. To say that no laws of a given type shall be made means that no laws of that type shall, under any circumstances, be made" 1948, 17). To Meiklejohn, the First Amendment is sacrosanct and the primary defense of intellectual freedom. Robert Downs, the distinguished University of Illinois librarian, synthesizes the First Amendment issue for libraries in his introduction to an essay by Ralph E. McCoy. "The most basic law protecting the freedom of speech and the press in America was the first amendment to be added to the U.S. Constitution--a recognition of its profound importance... The language is simple and implicit. Nevertheless, a sizeable segment of a library could be filled with judicial and other attempts to interpret the fundamental law, and often pervert its meaning. Controversy continues to swirl around the amendment as each age brings new points of view to bear upon it" (1984, 28).

On the other side of this debate, the forces that justify at least some form of censorship do not view their position as an anathema to the Constitution and democratic principles as their civil libertarian counterparts may view them. Numerous recorded incidents in censorship newsletters have quite often included quotes from the complainant that begin, "I'm against censorship, but..." or something similar. Many individuals act against one specific work to exercise what they see as parental rights or rights of a citizen while genuinely believing that they support the First Amendment. Others fear being labeled an extremist or "book burner."

Walter Berns, a distinguished scholar, is one voice that goes farther and advocates the need for censorship to protect morality and high standards of art and creativity. "Love needs privacy, which is one reason why the law forbids public sexual intercourse and forbade pornography. This is what it means to say that censorship, in trying to maintain the moral distinction between the nonobscene and the obscene, has the effect of maintaining the distinction between the human and the base, and therefore,...between art and trash" (1976, 215). However, rather than arguing for a replacement of First Amendment rights with a mechanism for social order set on enforcing morality, Berns believes civil libertarians have strayed from the original intent of the authors of the Constitution. "One looks in vain for a discussion of the problem of vulgar speech or of obscenity in the records of the Constitutional Convention of 1787 or in the *Federalist Papers* or in the debates in the First Congress on the First Amendment, which fact allowed Justice Douglas to jump to the conclusion that censorship of obscenity is a product of latter-day squeamishness, but from which it is more reasonable to conclude that the Founders took it for granted that obscenity was not constitutionally protected speech" (1979, 196). To those who oppose a more absolute position on intellectual freedom, the crux of the matter is not the protection of an ideal state of freedom, but the maintenance of high moral standards. This call for limitations on obscenity is not incompatible with civil liberties as these proponents view them because this form of censorship will protect democracy. Henry Clor states, "It is true that a free society seeks to contain the role of public authority and to provide broad scope for independent thought and action in such matters. But, though the role of public authority can be confined, it cannot be abolished; the latitude for freedom of thought and action can be broad, but it cannot be boundless" (1969, 200).

The controversies that arise because of censorship challenges are driven by this conflict between these polarized forces. Intellectual freedom advocates operate on a high philosophical plain and view censors as those who would destroy the ideals of the First Amendment. Those individuals and groups who challenge creative expression do not see themselves as censors, but as individuals exercising their rights as citizens and view civil libertarians as defenders of pornography that will destroy the moral fiber of the nation. Cal Thomas, vice-president of the Moral Majority (1983), even went so far as to turn the tables by calling civil libertarians, especially librarians, "book burners" because they ridicule conservative and Christian publications and do not balance library collections with these materials.

This conflict is a war of words, but one that has the potential for reordering how expression is created and disseminated. As with any war, there are combatants and noncombatants, those who get involved by design or by happenstance and those who avoid the problem, but, in this conflict, they are librarians, teachers, parents, authors, artists, politicians, students, children, celebrities, almost anyone, and none of these categories are exclusive to any side in the conflict. As with any army, these participants include generals, sergeants, and privates, and there are battle-scarred veterans as well as new recruits. The ability to use resources available and acquired expertise can be determined by the amount of experiences these individuals have encountered in their personal struggle to confront objections. Most intellectual freedom literature is intended to broaden the experiences of others and to add to the resources that can be used for facing challenges.

In this conflict, practitioners in the field are often looking for a better means for confronting censorship challenges. Anecdotes about censorship challenges are the mainstay of many articles on intellectual freedom and are one type of resource. These war stories, if you will, serve to enlighten those new to the profession or new to censorship problems and often provide quite practical advice on how to handle a challenge, especially when the circumstances are similar or the same. However, some librarians have experienced less success in applying these stories to their own situation. Often in the military, old sarges are viewed by new recruits as crusty old-timers whose stories are at once awesome experiences to be admired yet too unreal to apply to themselves. As with the military, new professionals can develop a sense of overconfidence, because such a reliance on anecdotes with successful endings is often a desire for an easy solution. Applying them in a given situation may work, but confronting censorship attacks involves too many possible contingencies in a charged political environment to be applicable in every situation.

Although the anecdote can be useful, the statistical method is also seen as a way to approach a problem. The anecdotes provide some information but not much in the way of useful empirical data. Statistics can provide quantitative data that may be useful from a broader perspective as well as for a given problem. But statistics alone are not a method for combatting challenges either. It is this argument that has driven the purpose of the following study. The anecdotal record and statistical analysis account for a significant portion of the literature on intellectual freedom. This study has also sprung from a commitment to combat censorship, a career of examining the theory and practice of intellectual freedom, and the fascination with the compilation of censorship incidents and data, most notably with L. B. Woods' 1979 study *A Decade of Censorship in America* and Lee Burress' 1989 book *Battle of the Books*, among many others. Both of these publications have an emphasis on statistical method and a record of significant data on the incidents of censorship.

Both of these approaches, anecdote and research, have value for the study of censorship and for the advocates of intellectual freedom. However, there are some substantial differences between them that have influenced the conduct of this study. The telling of a good story often has the richness of a life experience that reaches into the soul of an individual. It often sticks in the gray matter of the brain, to surface much later when triggered either for a retelling or for use in reflecting on a current experience. It is usually much more interesting to hear than a set of statistics.

Yet, as mentioned, the anecdote has some flaws. It is difficult to generalize to any other given situation, and possibly even deleterious. The evidence it presents may be purely circumstantial and only an unrepresentative snapshot of a problem. There are certain children who have the knack for making a sibling look like the guilty party, for example. The parent in these cases essentially gets a "snapshot" of the hapless child who has the misfortune of being in the wrong place at the wrong time, just after the truly guilty child disappears. The parent sees only the "anecdote," the child holding the smoking gun, but lacks the more accurate story. A statistic out of context is a similar "snapshot" that can be misused. The anecdotal record makes for good listening, but does not necessarily tell enough about the climate of censorship, what has caused the climate, what the elements that constitute it are, and how pervasive it is. Woods believed an empirical study was useful for at least four reasons:

1. The anecdotal record may repeat the same story giving an erroneous impression of a more grave situation than in reality, and a statistical study can help to avoid this.
2. A statistical study can provide more information on the subject of censorship.
3. Such a study can validate the level of censorship.
4. Statistical studies can provide the basis for further research (1979, 8).

A statistical approach is sometimes viewed as having little value for solving real, immediate difficulties. The use of a discrete piece of information, such as how many times *Slaughterhouse Five* was censored, is not readily seen as useful by a librarian who knows it is a vital novel for the age group but is faced with an angry school board member beholden to a powerful and/or vocal group, such as Citizens for Decency through Law or the Moral Majority. Although one such statistic alone may not be the answer, a statistical study, in total, may be of value to individual professionals and the profession in a number of ways:

1.   As with the anecdote, it can sensitize and serve as a point for advocacy.
2. It has shock value or the potential for shock value, especially if it reveals facts no one suspected.
3. It can be an alerting factor and help prepare professionals for possible challenges.
4. It can validate common knowledge or disprove myths about what is censored, how much is censored, by whom, and what happens to censored materials.
5. It can satisfy our curiosity about the climate of censorship.
6. It may be useful as part of a strategy in combatting a challenge.

There is a danger in a purely statistical course of action. Statistics as a rule are emotionless and valueless. There is nothing in a piece of data, per se, to indicate for instance, that a given number of censorship attempts is good or bad, although it may be said that many intellectual freedom advocates believe that just one challenge is a grave matter. The anecdotal record is filled with passion and takes a stand. It is so much more interesting to read or hear. The flat rendering of data, however, leaves it open to anyone as to its value and usefulness. The raw data may kick a sleeping dog and provide ammunition for the forces of censorship or may sway those who may teeter on the brink of the opposing side. It is not the intention of this book to be passionless. On the contrary, this statistical record is being compiled for the express purpose of aiding and abetting the cause of intellectual freedom.

Empirical research of censorship challenges is not new. Some of the more significant ones, Woods (1979) and Burress (1989), have been mentioned earlier and most of the studies are described in Chapter 2 of this book. However, there is a need to continue with more data collection and analysis. First, all such studies cover a limited time period and new research will provide insight into currently acquired information. It has been sixteen years since the publication of *A Decade of Censorship in America* and seven years since *Battle of the Books* was released, for example. Woods' data was compiled from one decade, 1966-1975, and Burress' surveys measured a monumental thirty-five years of data. Researchers cannot assume that censorship has ended or dwindled or that there is a lack of worthwhile data simply because it has been gathered before. On the contrary, new eras bring on more and different challenges. This work examines the Reagan-Bush era. As with Woods' study, it has measured the number and types of censorship challenges for one decade, 1981-1990. This overlaps the work of Burress by five years, but there is no duplication of the time periods of either Woods' original book nor his follow-up five-year study, published as an ERIC (Educational Resource Information Center) document. Although the first five years of data are for the same years as those reported in *Battle of the Books*, an entirely different methodology has been used than that of Burress. Furthermore, this decade as a distinct era has been viewed as important to research in and of itself. The election of Ronald Reagan in 1980 was heralded at the time by many conservatives (and feared by many liberals) as a major paradigm shift in the conduct of public life, and certainly of government. Conservatives of many stripes saw Reagan's assent to power as an opportunity to steer the nation back to a path of conservative values. One example of the dangers this foretold, touted by liberals, was the Reagan administration's foreign policy in regards to human rights abuses in other countries. In the early stages of Reagan's first year, David Rockefeller was sent on a mission to Latin American states to assure those governments of a more accommodationist policy on human rights than the Carter administration. Jacobo Timerman, an Argentine journalist imprisoned and tortured by the military government of Argentina from 1977 to 1979, denounced Reagan's "quiet diplomacy," for example, and became a center of controversy between U.S. conservatives and liberals on this issue.

On the home front, the Reagan election signaled the fear of increased censorship challenges committed by emboldened right-wing groups, particularly the Moral Majority, which appeared to be a moving force within the Reagan circle. In the spring of 1981, the North Carolina chapter of the Moral Majority released a report on school textbooks, curriculum, and library materials and vowed to mobilize parents throughout the state to rid the schools of inappropriate materials. Within a year, the Washington State chapter of the Moral Majority demanded that the state library turn over circulation records on two films, one on abortion, it found objectionable in an attempt to gather data to ban them. In 1986, Reagan appointed James Dobson, founder of Focus on the Family, to the Attorney General's Commission on Pornography and Obscenity. Two national textbook controversies of the late 1980s involved conservative fundamentalist groups: Concerned Women for America in Churchill, Tennessee, in 1986 and the Christian Broadcasting Network in an Alabama textbook case in 1989.

Another value in gathering statistics is the ability to forecast, which involves the analysis of trends in data reported. One of the drawbacks in a statistical forecast comes from the nature of forecasting. Like a weather forecast, it can be wrong because of an unexpected turn of events. As an example, Woods (1979) suggested that his data "points to a more hard-line approach to acceptability or unacceptability of library and classroom materials." This may not have actually happened in the 1980s. Subsequent empirical studies can not only make their own forecasts but also confirm or nullify previous trend analyses and forecasts.

Research designs can vary from one study to the next and can fall short for several reasons. The design itself is usually unable to account for all possible influencing factors or variables. In the development of the research methodology, these uncontrolled variables are supposed to be controlled with statistical measures such as sample size. Regardless of how they are controlled, it is recognized that the universe one attempts to describe cannot usually be measured with complete accuracy. A new study can improve on an earlier design and account for different variables that were not included or accounted for in the previous study. Also, errors in data collection and analysis can be made on any piece of research, and new researchers can improve on the performance of an earlier work. Many scholars are aware of the need for continuing research in their field of endeavor. Woods (1979), for example, saw the value of the results of his work as the basis for further research in the field of intellectual freedom.

Following the example of the work done by Woods, this book is designed to search for answers to ten basic questions by examining reports of censorship incidents for the decade 1981-1990:

1. What is the total amount of materials and other forms of expression that were challenged in some way?
2. What are the titles of the censored materials? Because censorship challenges are often aimed at specific items, and most often books and textbooks, films, plays, periodicals, and newspapers with a distinct title, this question attempts to discover those materials most frequently mentioned. However, forms of expression lacking a clearly stated title are also included.
3. What are the types of expression that were challenged including, books and textbooks, periodicals and newspapers, film and videos, speakers, television and radio programs, music and dance, art, and computer files and networks?

4. What is the level of activity of censorship challenges in each year of the decade studied? When was the greatest number of challenges? When was the least number?

5. Where did the challenge occur? The study is designed to measure, by state, where the climate of censorship is the most difficult and where it is the least problematical.

6. What types of institutions have experienced challenges to materials and other forms of expression? The study is designed to measure not only libraries and educational institutions but also any other institution affected by a censorship attempt, such as museums, bookstores, theaters, television and radio stations or networks, publishers, and public forums.

7. Where did the challenges originate? Who are the individuals, types of individuals, or groups most often associated with a censorship incident? Are there any individuals or groups who on the surface appear to eschew censorship or seem to be unlikely to challenge a form of expression, but in fact sometimes or often do complain about content or other questionable issues?

8. What do the complainants see are cause for challenges to these materials? What constitutes the major sources of objections to expression and those sources of objections by type of material?

9. What are the outcomes of the challenges? A challenge begins with a complaint, but the outcome could be any one of many different possibilities. This study is designed to measure whether or not institutions are basically successful in combatting censorship complaints.

10. Who are the advocates for the materials or for intellectual freedom? Which groups or what individuals or types of individuals most often stand up for a book or other type of material? Who challenges the logic and veracity of the complainant?

Of these ten questions, nine are similar to those Woods used for his book. However, there are two major differences in this research design. A tenth question on the advocates of intellectual freedom has been added. This study seeks to answer not only who has complained about materials but also who has been willing to stand up to those challenges. Second, this work does not limit itself to educational institutions nor to a narrow range of formats of expression. All reports of censorship have been considered and inclusion is based on the following guidelines.

The guidelines for inclusion emphasize the nature of a challenge. A challenge, for the purpose of this study, is any complaint made to any owner, distributor, or repository of any form of identifiable expression. The challenge is not limited to an eventual act of censorship such as a ban, removal of an item, rejection of an item, or expurgation of it in any form, but simply if a complaint has been voiced to an authority, agency, or other holder of that form of expression. The content of the expressive form had to be the center of the complaint, although in some cases, a complaint was reported without a reason given. These incidents have been included, but recorded as "no reason given." Issues regarding the Freedom of Information Act and the free flow of information that have not originated from a content-based complaint, as well as religious freedom, the right to assembly, and reporters' privileges incidents, have not been included as well.

The ultimate desire of most publications critical of censorship is to maximize the freedom of expression in some manner. The purpose of a statistical compilation and analysis such as this book is to provide anyone interested in combatting censorship with another means of meeting these challenges and to present them with an objective measure for that cause. The value of a study on censorship can only be gauged by its impact on those who utilize it. There is a substantial body of literature on intellectual freedom. Many of these publications are filled with passionate discourse and many include at least some form of useful data. A comparison of the more statistically oriented books and articles follows to assist in evaluating the empirical data of this work and the study of censorship in general.

2   Censorship Literature

Anyone investigating the literature of censorship will likely be astounded by the vast body of writings on the subject. In June 1993 an online search of *Library Literature* using the subject term "censorship" produced a whopping 890 items published between the years 1984 and 1993. Likewise, a search for the descriptor "censorship" in the ERIC database delivered 822 records between 1982 and 1992. Obviously this is an important subject in the modern collective conscience, particularly in the minds of librarians and educators. Yet dealing with such a mountain of information can be a daunting task. Therefore, it is important to examine the literature for characteristic qualities or trends, to tease out of the great mass some understanding of the objectives, methods, and ideologies of all these writers.

Unfortunately, very little of the writing on censorship can be described as "research." It is largely anecdotal or polemical in nature, or both. In 1977 Richard E. McKee observed that "the existing body of theory and knowledge about this phenomenon is weak" (p. 193). Despite many public assertions about the growing importance of intellectual freedom issues in the 1980s, the nature of our knowledge has not changed much over the past decade and a half.

Yet many people still speak and write about the "climate of censorship" in our times, claiming growing tendencies to stifle this thought or that idea. Opinions from the entire range of the political spectrum are represented in these debates, and many of the arguments are well-fashioned. In *Liberty Denied* (1988) Donna A. Demac laments the rise of censorship in public schools, the publishing industry, and even our government. She uses many examples, from assaults on textbooks by the religious right to the Reagan administration's privatization of government information. William Noble (1990) makes largely the same arguments and observations, if only with different examples (including his own story of having a manuscript about a Chilean housing project rejected by a U.S. government-sponsored publication because of positive comments about Chile). The articles in *Freedom at Risk* (Curry 1988) present a similar litany of offenses by the Reagan administration--an overactive sense of national security, cutbacks in government printing, and assaults on the right to privacy.

If it seems these examples are all charges from the political left on their enemies to the right, one need not look far to find other writings with the roles reversed. Dinesh D'Souza's *Illiberal Education* (1991) is one of the more notable of these. Taking a page from William F. Buckley from thirty years before (see "The Superstitions of 'Academic Freedom'" in *God and Man at Yale*, 1951), D'Souza sees in American higher education a tendency to protect politically liberal ideas and attack the conservative. Affirmative action and gender equality are two issues he believes have become objects of extreme liberal orthodoxy, leaving little room for dissenting opinions among students and faculty. "Such hostility to free expression in the name of race and gender sensitivities is now the norm, not the exception, on the American campus" (1991, 144). This "new censorship," as he calls it, creates an environment of "political correctness" in our universities that stifles the free exchange of ideas. But, although this may not be an easily measured phenomenon, D'Souza, like his liberal counterparts, offers little more than a few narrative examples as his evidence.

In *Book Burning* (1983), a somewhat more extensively documented argument, Cal Thomas of the Moral Majority criticizes the supposed liberal bias of our media and educational machinery. Why is it, he asks, that Christian books and programs encounter such difficulty in their production and dissemination? In Thomas' judgment, the defenders of civil liberties hypocritically allow pornography to flourish while attacking the rights of the Christian faithful. Ironically though, the solution Thomas endorses, the religious freedom he seems to defend most vehemently, is the right to inhibit the production of opposing viewpoints: one censorship deserves another.

Writings from the library profession, although definitely advocating intellectual freedom, have tended to steer a course somewhere down the political middle of this war-torn road. Thus materials from the library world, when not simply presenting examples of particular censorship incidents, have often taken the form of a librarian's defense manual. What kind of censorship can one expect? Who is most likely to challenge materials? How can one successfully deal with challenges? The *Intellectual Freedom Manual* from the American Library Association is the most significant of these. It presents the association's official position, a political manifesto, if you will, on intellectual freedom and gives some history and interpretation of the position. *Defending Intellectual Freedom*, by Eli M. Oboler (1980), provides more concrete examples of how censorship occurs and a context for fighting it. From the teaching profession, *Dealing with Censorship* (edited by James E. Davis 1979), serves a similar function. The collection of essays entitled *Libraries, Erotica and Pornography* (edited by Martha Cornog 1991) presents the views of those both for and against library erotica, examines the problems involved in collecting such materials, and discusses the most relevant censorship issues.

INTELLECTUAL FRAMEWORK

Despite the advocacy of intellectual freedom within the library community, we are still without a strong theoretical and philosophical background for our position; we adhere to a largely unexamined belief system. Obviously, contemporary thinking on equality and personal liberty rests on the shoulders of the "Three Johns" of intellectual freedom: Milton, Locke, and Mill. Their work greatly informs much of our current discourse.

The poet John Milton, the most anomalous of the three, gives an impassioned plea for freedom of the press in his *Areopagitica* (1985). This work, addressed to the English Parliament, speaks for a free market of ideas: "when complaints are freely heard, deeply consider'd, and speedily reform'd, then is the utmost bound of civil liberty attain'd" p. 197). When his Puritan faith might have led him to think otherwise, Milton spoke strongly for the freedom to reason and argue publicly about government, morality, and even religion.

John Locke thought and wrote extensively on individual freedom; his ideas have come to us in more or less pure pedigree through the Declaration of Independence and the U.S. Constitution. For example, in his essay on civil government (the so-called "Second Treatise") (1989) he states that men (his term) are born with "an uncontrouled enjoyment of all the Rights and Priviledges of the Law of Nature, equally with any other Man . . . to preserve his Property, that is, his Life, Liberty, and Estate, against the Injuries and Attempts of other Men" (1989, 323). But like Milton, he also endorses a society that tolerates a variety of opinions:

If a Roman Catholic believe that to be really the body of Christ, which another man calls bread, he does no injury thereby to his neighbour. If a Jew do not believe the New Testament to be the Word of God, he does not thereby alter anything in men's civil rights. If a heathen doubt of both Testaments, he is not therefore to be punished as a pernicious citizen. ("A Letter Concerning Toleration," p. 205)

John Mill, in *On Liberty*, sees as reason enough for free and open inquiry the possibility of human fallibility:

for while every one well knows himself to be fallible, few think it necessary to take any precautions against their own fallibility, or admit the supposition that any opinion, of which they feel is certain, may be one of the examples of the error to which they acknowledge themselves to be liable. (1989, 21)

Thus freedom of thought and speech can protect us from the error of certainty. This is an argument that is not readily acceptable to those who believe their truth is received through divine intervention--God is never wrong.

Mill offers four main reasons to maintain a vigorous free market of ideas. First, a suppressed idea may be true. Second, an idea may be, if not wholly true, at least partly true or capable of pointing toward truth. Third, even true ideas will be received with prejudice and lack of understanding, if they are not allowed to be contested. This can lead, finally, to the possibility that the idea will become nothing more than dogma and in the process lose some of its meaning entirely.

In the library world today, the two documents that hold the greatest influence over our thoughts on intellectual freedom--our Declaration of Independence and Constitution, if you will--are the "Library Bill of Rights" (note the reference to the U.S. Constitution) and "The Freedom to Read" statement, both from the American Library Association. The" Bill of Rights" dates from 1938, and "Freedom to Read " statement from 1953. Of course these position statements have not been formed without a great deal of discussion and thinking, but most librarians today have only vague notions about what they say and mean, and a fair number do not even hold them in high regard (note, for example, the recent row over gay rights that took place in the pages of *American Libraries*, or some of the research findings discussed later in this chapter).

The foremost thought in the "Library Bill of Rights" is that libraries and librarians should play an important role in the free market of ideas, fostering a diversity of opinions and materials, and fighting any attempts at censorship. "Libraries should challenge censorship in the fulfillment of their responsibility to provide information and enlightenment" (Article 2, *Intellectual Freedom Manual*, 19,3). The "Freedom to Read" statement goes on to endorse this concept and to further defend the rights of publishers, authors, and readers alike against any attacks, even those based on societal well-being or moral certainty. "We realize that the application of these propositions may mean the dissemination of ideas and manners of expression that are repugnant to many persons" (19, 111).

In the recent literature, an issue of *Library Trends* offers a few of the more sophisticated philosophical discussions of intellectual freedom. David V. Ward (1990) examines the nature of "rights" and applies these thoughts to several censorship examples. In ethical theory, he explains, "rights" fall into two main groups, deontological theories and consequentialist theories. These conform generally to the positions of Locke and Mill, respectively. The consequentialist theory of rights is utilitarian in nature; if something produces good consequences, it is said to represent a "right" (see again Mill's four reasons for maintaining vigorous public discussion of ideas). In deontological theories, on the other hand, our rights are obtained independently from the good they may create. This can best be represented by the "inalienable rights" that form the basis of U.S. government. The "Founding Fathers" recognized these types of rights not because of their utilitarian nature (although that would be a pleasant byproduct), but just because they are "inalienable" or "god-given." Deontological rights correspond directly with Locke's "Rights and Priviledges of the Law of Nature."

A deontological approach has almost always taken legal ascendancy over utilitarian rights in our society. Objectors to pornography, for example, may point rationally to the anti-social behavior and hatred of women these materials allegedly generate, but they have rarely been able to overthrow in court the right of producers to produce or consumers to consume. On the other hand, Ward (1990) points out that deontological rights cannot be applied universally to all library situations. An author, for example, does not have the "right" to have his or her book purchased by every library in the world--no individual's rights are necessarily violated if a library does not own particular materials. In fact, taxpayers are within their rights to determine what materials to place in their publicly funded libraries. This is one of the limits of deontological rights. However, in the consequentialist model, it may be beneficial to have a variety of viewpoints, ideas, and cultures represented in the library collection. "The librarian," as Ward notes, "is in a special position to aid the public in understanding that, while it has the *right* to remove or ban books from publicly supported institutions, doing so is *unwise*. Such removals are wrong and constitute bad public policy just because the long-term consequences may be disastrous" (1990, 84).

R. Kathleen Molz explores another binary aspect of intellectual freedom: the relationship between what she calls regulative and existential censorship. Regulative censorship involves those cases we most often think of in the library profession--challenges to materials that offend some orthodoxy or belief system. Existential censorship is much more difficult to observe or measure, and involves "monopolistic domination by either the state or the market to subvert or deny public access to some forms of knowledge and information" (1990, 20). As Michael H. Harris (1984) has noted, this type of censorship can exert an almost hegemonic control over our behavior, completely disallowing some ways of thinking; even librarians may be powerless to resist its influence.

Molz implies that changes in government administrations may dictate the nature of our "regime values"--the system of political beliefs we follow. As regime values change, different types of existential censorship come into play, and different regulative censorship may become more common. In the administrations of Ronald Reagan and George Bush, Molz sees some relationship to the growing public tendency to subvert individual freedoms, a relationship between the surveillance methods of the FBI's Library Awareness Program, for example, and the public urge to inhibit access to some types of materials by some members of society. Government programs may suggest the appropriateness of certain behaviors in public.

SURVEYING CENSORSHIP

It has been established that censorship is a compelling and sensitive issue for the intellectuals of our day, that it is--at least--a topic worthy of discussion in many different arenas. Therefore, if we are to discuss the topic with any degree of authority there must be significant research to refer to, there must be data available to reinforce our views, information on which to base our conclusions. Since we find it necessary to talk about the nature and level of censorship taking place today as part of our cultural and social critique, there must be some measure of those variables available. Unfortunately, these conclusions receive little reinforcement in the literature. For all the importance intellectual freedom is granted in our literature, little effort has been expended in gauging the levels of censorship or measuring any of the social variables involved.

In reviewing the literature up to 1979, Judith Serebnick provides an excellent framework for analyzing studies of censorship and suggests areas in need of future research. "To explain and predict censorship in libraries, it may be necessary to deviate from primary or exclusive focus on librarian variables and rather to examine the additional classes of independent variables .... Problems of censorship in libraries usually occur in the context of larger problems, local and national, and it is doubtful that they can be explained adequately without investigating institutional and societal influences" (1979,115).

Because much of it is done by librarians and library professionals, censorship research has indeed tended to revolve around the library and its constituents. One of the main tools of this type of research has been the survey, and because the universe of librarians is a somewhat known quantity, they have tended to be the chosen subject of many such measurement instruments.

Several major studies have used the survey instrument as a way of gauging librarians' attitudes about censorship and preselection and correlating these to other variables--demographic, personal, and professional. One of the first and most significant of these was done by Marjorie Fiske and published in 1959 (later reissued in 1968). Fiske avoided one of the major pitfalls of surveys--poor response rate--by conducting interviews in person with 204 librarians and administrators in both public and school settings in California. Her major finding is that librarians, although they voiced strong support of intellectual freedom, tend to censor themselves by being very selective when choosing among materials they thought might be sensitive. Another striking discovery is that librarians have a low self-image within their institutions, and that this tends to affect the way they deal with challenges to materials.

Charles H. Busha (1972) conducted a similar mail survey of 900 Midwestern public librarians and had a 69% usable response rate. Along with attitudes toward intellectual freedom, Busha also attempted to gauge the librarians' authoritarian beliefs based on a system of measurement developed by T. W. Adorno. The most disturbing finding in this study is the gulf between librarian rhetoric and action; Busha sees very little variation among librarians' level of support for intellectual freedom and the "Library Bill of Rights," but great variation in their willingness to actually take part in censorial activities. As might be expected, those librarians with greater authoritarian beliefs are more willing to censor. Some other correlations Busha noted are that older librarians tend to accept censorship more readily than younger colleagues, and that opposition to censorship increases with greater levels of education.

In a nationwide study, Michael Pope (1974) surveyed school, public, and academic librarians for their attitudes toward selecting sexually oriented materials. Although the questionnaire was extensively pre-tested, a response rate of only 59% was all that was achieved. In this study several categories of sexually oriented materials were presented to the librarians as possible library selections, and they were asked to pick a response that would best describe how they would deal with the material.

Although school librarians are the most likely to reject any sexually oriented material, academic librarians may have been hiding their opposition behind the "wait until faculty request" response. Likewise, all the librarians may have found it easy to couch their offense to certain materials in terms of the "appropriateness" for the audience. Overall, women are more likely to reject sensitive materials than men, but this may have been a factor of their greater numbers in the school librarian ranks. In looking at librarians' undergraduate backgrounds, it has been found that science majors are the most restrictive and social science majors the least; humanities majors fall in between. As in Busha's study, greater education correlates with less restrictive behavior (Pope 1974). Interestingly, the existence of a library selection policy has little relationship to the practices of the subjects.

A number of studies have attempted to use the survey as a method of gauging not only librarians' attitudes but also the general level of censorship activity taking place and some of its more prevalent characteristics. One of the problems with using a survey to collect factual data, as Algin M. Schrader noted in his 1989 article, is the reliance the surveyor must place on the memory and truthfulness of the subjects. Schrader and his research partners tried to alleviate this problem by focusing on recent events and limiting their study to a three-year period.

This project, an examination of censorship incidents in college and research libraries of the Canadian Prairie Provinces, reveals some interesting findings. Just as with most school and public libraries, sexually oriented materials are the objects of most challenges. Smaller schools tend to have more challenges than larger schools. Strangely, the data on the effectiveness of selection policies in fighting challenges is inconclusive. The most startling finding of this survey is that librarians or other library employees are involved at some point in the initiation of 40% of the challenges, a substantial amount of the total. These include incidents where the library staff either initiated the challenge themselves or were in agreement with the challenge and signed on with the objector, but excludes those in which the librarian simply capitulated in the end to the censor's demands.

Schrader (1992) also conducted a nationwide survey of Canadian public libraries. For whatever reasons, this study only elicited a 56% response rate from the subjects. Similar to the findings of other studies, it revealed that about one third of the libraries experienced some kind of challenge, but that in 70% of these cases the questionable material has been retained. Of the over 500 titles challenged, most have just one objection lodged, pointing to the capricious nature of most challenges and the impossibility of predicting what might give offense. As might be expected, children's reading rights are the most at risk in these public libraries.

Another interesting finding is that only 4% of the challenges were reported in any kind of public media. Thus, the vast majority of challenges are taking place behind closed doors. It might be interesting to determine why this is so. Is it the objector or the librarian who wants to keep things quiet? If it is the librarian, are they protecting the reputation of the objector or the reputation of the library? Is librarianship simply a profession that shuns controversy? Would a greater public airing of library challenges be of benefit to the censor or the library? These are questions for which it might serve us well to find the answers.

In 1981, the Association of American Publishers, in conjunction with the American Library Association and the Association for Supervision and Curriculum Development, published the results of a nationwide survey they had conducted of teachers, administrators, and school librarians. The aim of this particular project was to measure the censorship climate within the public education environment in toto. Along with the survey results, a list of the most censored titles was provided. The survey summary, *Limiting What Students Shall Read*, written by Michelle Marder Kamhi (1981), reinforces the findings of may other studies. Accordingly, about one third of libraries experience challenges. Only 15% of these challenges are reported in the media. It was also found that collection development policies can be effective tools in dealing with challenges.

There are some unique findings reported by Kamhi as well. Most challenges to textbook adoption are initiated by groups or organizations rather than individuals. Groups affiliated with the "New Right" were, at that time, playing a larger and larger role in challenging school and library materials. The most significant observation this report makes is that educators and librarians are ineffective in communicating their educational objectives and the rationale for using particular materials to the public; contact with the community about the curriculum rarely takes place *before* a challenge is lodged.

Diane McAfee Hopkins studied the censorship phenomenon extensively and presents her findings in a number of recent articles. Following some of Serebnick's suggestions, Hopkins uses surveys of librarians and administrators to study the variables involved in challenges, retention, and removal. The first article in this series (1989) presents a theoretical model of the elements that influence the outcome of a challenge, a model that resembles the Shannon-Wiener representation of the communication process, where there is (1) a sender or transmitter, (2) a message, (3) a receiver of the message, and (4) any noise that may inhibit full transmission. In Hopkins' theory, the simplicity of a single conduit of information flow is complicated by the input of data from many sources: the challenger, librarian, community, administration, and so on. One phenomenon Hopkins recognizes as a possible problem in resisting censorship attempts is what she and other scholars have called the "Spiral of Silence." This describes the tendency to remain silent when one perceives that popular opinion, either internal or external to the institution, runs counter to one's own views. In Hopkins' second published report (1990), the finding that only 13% of challenges are reported in the media closely matches the results of other studies and reiterates the notion that most censorship is taking place behind closed doors.

The outcomes of Hopkins' research replicates in some form several other studies in relation to the variables of a censorship incident. For instance, about one in three libraries will have experienced some censorship pressure. Also, selection policies are useful in defending library material. As reported in an article in 1993, one variation from other censorship studies is that librarian "self-esteem" does not strongly correlate to censorship success. What is more significant is the "locus of control" in making library decisions and the librarian's willingness to follow a dogmatic administrator. In the whole complex of interrelations, she has found that retention of materials depends on the existence of a selection policy and support both externally and internally for the retention decision. Nonretention depends on who the principal initiator is, librarian submissiveness, librarian commitment to a closed belief system, and general support for the removal decision.

Hopkins suggests that schools and school media specialists try to communicate more openly with the public about educational goals to promote stronger external support for school programs. She also recommends educating media specialists and potential media specialists about the nature of the challenges they are likely to face in their careers.

Lee Burress has also conducted a number of censorship surveys. His work has usually centered around works of literature and the experiences of English teachers with censorship attempts. The emphasis has normally been placed on the "who" and "what" of censorship and less on the precise measurement of variables leading to successful resistance, which Hopkins has so effectively studied. Nonetheless, his work does present an interesting snapshot of what censors think of contemporary literature.

As an example of Burress' methods, let us look briefly at his 1979 survey report published by the National Council of Teachers of English. This study drew a sample of 2,000 teachers to be surveyed. Unfortunately, the response rate was only 38%. Perhaps one of the problems with this survey is that it asked a daunting number of questions and the layout of the questionnaire was rather confusing. For example, several questions were posed about challenges to different types of materials (books, journals, school papers, etc.), but for each of these types, space for only three incidents was all that was given. This might, in effect, have told the subjects that no more than three incidents should be reported. Although the surveys were sent to English teachers, some of the questions might have been more appropriate for the librarian, but only two questions instructed the subjects to seek the librarian's assistance.

The major findings of this survey are in line with what other scholars have found. Sex and bad language, as always, top the list of reasons for objections. About 30% of the respondents have experienced some challenge to reading materials. In the environment under examination here--public schools--parents, as might be expected, are the initiators of the greatest number of challenges. Student publications, it has also been found, are highly susceptible to control and censorship.

Burress' *Battle of the Books* (1989) is made up mostly of a discussion of the censorship issues he has observed over the years, but an appendix also presents a list of challenged titles drawn from seventeen different surveys conducted in various parts of the United States between 1963 and 1984. These surveys do not necessarily cover the entire country for that time period, and the accumulation, in fact, raises questions of their compatibility. Because of the capricious nature of challenges to materials, any list, no matter how long, is not necessarily a complete index of all objectionable titles.

MEASURING THE MEDIA

Few options exist, other than surveys, for measuring levels of censorship. Many people have decried the absence of a nationwide index to track the ebb and flow of the censorial urge, but to date no such tool exists. The closest possible candidate is the database the American Library Association's Office for Intellectual Freedom has begun compiling. This is not publicly available, and we must, therefore, rely on other methods. Several Intellectual Freedom organizations now monitor incidents and publish lists and statements about how they view the current climate. These include the American Library Association's *Newsletter on Intellectual Freedom* and the People for the American Way's *Attacks on the Freedom to Learn, Censorship News*, published by the National Coalition Against Censorship, and the *Student Press Law Center Report*, produced by the organization of the same name. Since these four periodicals provide most of the data of this research and are monitored frequently, they are referred to in this text either by their full title as above or in abbreviated form. The *Newsletter on Intellectual Freedom* is also listed as *NIF* or *Newsletter*. The *Attacks on the Freedom to Learn* is also labeled *ATFL*. *Censorship News* is often simply listed as *CN* whereas the *Student Press Law Center Report* is also listed as *SPLC* or *SPLC Report*. Each describes a number of challenges to books and other materials from throughout the United States and some foreign countries. Most of the information is derived from newspaper reports gathered by the organizations. *NIF* is the more extensive of the four, but with the knowledge that only a small percentage of challenges are reported in the media, it must be considered a sample of the entire censorship universe.

Several studies have used *NIF* as a source of data on censorship. This approach has a number of benefits and drawbacks.   Questions about the reliability of the survey subjects are replaced by questions of the news report. Often the reports will not contain enough data on all the variables to make a valuable analysis of relationships.   *NIF* does present a greater picture of censorship in the United States than it is possible to get from most surveys.

The best-known study that is based on information gathered from *NIF* is *A Decade of Censorship in America* by L. B. Woods. This study examines all types of incidents reported in the *Newsletter* between the years 1966 and 1975. The book sets out to answer nine major questions about censorship in the 1960s and 1970s. To summarize briefly: When, where, how many, and what formats of material are challenged? What are the titles of challenged material? What types of institutions are involved?   Who has initiated the attempts and for what reasons? What are the final dispositions?

Woods uses his data to track the rise and fall of challenges through the decade and to give an index of censorship activity for each state in the United States. This index is a factor of the state population and the number of challenges. He also presents a number of tables that track variables such as the affiliations of the challenge initiators. One shortcoming of this study is that Woods does little analysis of correlation between variables. Data is usually presented as a simple tabulation of totals and percentages. It does, however, give a useful look at the kinds of materials that gave offense in the 1960s and 1970s.

Woods himself took part in a number of studies that continued to use a similar analysis covering the years up to 1980.   In a paper of 1982 with Cynthia Robinson, he reports that the number of censorship incidents had declined in the late 1970s, but that he expected an increase during the 1980s. These findings are backed up by a similarly conducted study published in 1986 by the National Commission on Libraries and Information Science covering the years 1975 to 1985. In examining *NIF* reports, this study found that incidents fell until 1979 and then rose to a high in 1982 then dropped slightly until 1985. The total number of titles challenged has shown similar fluctuations, but has continued to rise beyond the 1982 levels. School libraries, it has been found, experienced the greatest number of complaints and were the most likely to capitulate to the censor's demands.

In looking at the literature, it is clear that a concern for the level of censorship activity and a desire for some concrete measurement is widespread.   But although this concern is prevalent, very few scholars have undertaken the task of monitoring the intellectual freedom environment. This is perhaps because of the difficulty of the project. Those who will attempt such an analysis have few tools at their command, fewer sources of data, and little philosophical framework to guide them. But it is challenges like this that can inspire us to strive for changes--changes in our own professional literature, but, more importantly, changes in the attitudes of people, attitudes that affect how they might interact with views they find unpleasant, disagreeable, or offensive.

3 Methodology

This study is a measurement of censorship complaints over a ten year period, 1981-1990, reported in four different reporting sources. In order to obtain an accurate measurement, this research hinges on what constitutes a challenge or complaint. The definition of a complaint is crucial in determining what should be measured and what should not. Although some may see a difference between a "challenge" and a "complaint," the two are viewed as synonymous in this design. The nature of a complaint, however, is generally defined here as any question or objection to an intellectually created work or speech, whether verbally conveyed or written, made to the creator or owner of the work or to an authoritative body with some responsibility for its existence or use. This is a broadly based concept because censorship is a phenomena with far-reaching impact in society and the desire is to be as inclusive as possible in its measurement. However, this more inclusive supposition presents some issues of dispute between an absolutist view of intellectual freedom and the belief that some form of censorship is legitimate in order to understand the application of this definition.

Nat Hentoff (1992), a well-known advocate for intellectual freedom, recently wrote a book entitled, *Free Speech for Me But Not for Thee: How the American Left and Right Relentlessly Censor Each Other*. He contends that both liberals and conservatives insist that their actions are virtuous principle, not censorship, while their ideological other-half, instead, is the true censor. In other words, what is one person's complaint is another's rightful viewpoint. Differing philosophies or approaches to intellectual freedom, then, cause disagreements as to what constitutes a valid or true complaint. Librarians are often faced with a similar charge of bias in selection of materials from conservative groups, and sometimes their own, over selection practices. Phyllis Schafly and Cal Thomas, for example, often accuse librarians of censoring conservative publications, such as those published by the Moral Majority or written from a pro-life perspective, for not including these books in collections (see Cal Thomas *Book*

Burning (1983). This issue often revolves around what constitutes selection. Is a decision not to buy *Playboy* or *Show Me!* for a library, for example, a decision that recognizes the mission of the institution or a product of the established selection criteria, or a fear that it will be destroyed or stolen soon after it is acquired or does it result from a belief that the pictures are obscene or too sexually explicit? In many similar selection decisions, no true answer is ever known. Selection can be based on personal bias or even personal whim, which a professional may not be willing to reveal. In selection instances of this nature, the complaint can be an unspoken or hidden one.

The question arises as to what constitutes censorship if a definition of a complaint is to be formulated. Reichman defines censorship as "the removal, suppression or restricted circulation of literary, artistic, or educational materials of images, ideas, and information on the grounds that these are morally or otherwise objectionable in light of standards applied by the censor" (1988, 2). This definition implies that something is actually done that either prohibits use entirely or in part; that the censored item is no longer available in an unfettered manner. As Reichman states, some theories argue that this can only occur under the auspices of a governing authority and that a citizen complaint does not constitute censorship. This is an argument often made by individuals accused of censorship activities. The rationale is that citizens have a constitutional right to redress grievances and present concerns to government and their agents about the perceived harmful effects such expressive efforts can cause. The contention is that the legitimate exercise of such rights is not censorship, only actions taken by legal authorities can be so labeled. In other words, according to this argument, a complaint does not equal censorship and challenges of this nature do not necessarily count as complaints.

The logic of this viewpoint, however, relies on the assumption that there is a benign link between the legitimate complaint and the act of censorship. In other words, even though a complaint was made and the authority censored the work, the complaint, due to its legitimacy, was not responsible for the censorship. But as Reichman observes, "pressures exerted by private citizens or citizen groups can also result in removal or suppression of 'objectionable' items" (1988, 2). Such pressure connects citizens with the governing body because in a political environment, the two groups rely on each other's support directly and indirectly, with political power holding the alliances together. Censorship controversies threaten, at the very least, political stability, which is most often a factor in a decision to censor by the authorities.

The link between complaint and censorship act can be more readily understood with a classification of the types of possible complaints. The challenges accumulated for this research can be categorized into four groups that demonstrate the full spectrum of the gross catalytic effect of citizen pressure to censorship act. This spectrum runs the gamut from no apparent connection to total, direct action at the hands of the complainants themselves. In the first category, which can be called "benign complaint," where the pressure exerted appears to have no effect, the complaints appear not to threaten the governing authority's decision. For example, if parents file a formal complaint with a school, follow the proper procedures in completing the required forms, and do not challenge the ultimate decision when it weighs against them, then the fact that an act of censorship occurred is questionable. In several recorded incidents, the literature lists cases where the review procedure for citizen complaints was followed with no adverse effect on the expressive work that was subject to question. In other instances, the complaint was first made, then withdrawn. A few reports indicated that an informal complaint or off-hand comment was rendered without any action taken or negative ramification. On the surface, the types of complaints in this category appear to validate the assumption that there is a benign link, and, therefore, cannot be legitimately counted as censorship. However, the potential for censorship of the work exists because over time, there is no guarantee that the complaint would end at this stage. There is also the possibility of a "chilling effect," which is discussed later.

In the second category of challenges, the complaint is made but denied, but the complainant acts in such a way that threatens further action. Because of the polarization between complainant and governing authority, this category can be labeled "non-consensus complaints." The link between complaint and action is more apparent, although no censorship occurs, but there is potential for a suppression of the work. However, although the pressure is applied both during the complaint stage and after a decision not to censor occurs, the benign link between the challenge and any potential act of censorship is still apparent. The assumption that no connection exists is made on the basis that despite pressure exerted, the governing body acted on their own conscience. At this stage, the complaint could go further but has only resulted in a difference in the course of the complaint between complainant and governing authority. This research discovered numerous instances wherein a complaint was filed, properly or extra-legally, or voiced in some way, but the agency publicly refused to censor the item or took a formal vote against the complaint. In these cases, the complainant publicly denounced the decision, threatened further action and/or challenged the authority in some way; that is, called for the authority's resignation or for voters to remove them from office. The link is not benign in this instance because the governing body faces a challenge that has the potential for censorship as well as for destabilizing the governing authority.

The third category of complaints demonstrates the direct influence of citizen pressure on censorship action. In these situations, once the citizen complaint is made, the governing body censors the item in question in some way because they agree with the complaint. Because the authority acts upon the complaint after some consideration, this category can be labeled "consensus complaints." For those individuals who accept the theory that only official authorities censor, the censorship act is not a result of the complaint made but a result of the decision process of the governing body. The data gathering of this study recorded numerous instances wherein such actions were taken out of fear that negative consequences would be destructive for the institution, or that a loss of personal position or change in or the elimination of that institution would occur, in addition to a conscientious review of the facts. This category demonstrates that indeed private individuals and groups function as true and effective censors because of their political power influence.

Although the level of complaints, as just outlined, can be seen as the total in possible action taken by individuals, a fourth and more disturbing category exists that is a full realization of censorship action taken by private citizens rather than just by an official authority. Many censorship incidents can be found in the literature wherein direct citizen action culminated in an overt act of censorship. In some cases, the objectionable book or item was stolen or checked out and never returned. In other instances, the item was vandalized or destroyed beyond repair. Such actions were not only direct, they also bypassed legally established channels for redressing grievances through a formal review. Because of the destructive nature of these challenges, this category can be called "radical complaints." These acts must be seen as a type of vigilantism that threatens the foundation of democracy by what Alexis de Tocqueville called "a tyranny of the majority," or what might be more properly called in many cases a "tyranny of the minority."

As this review of these four categories of complaints, has shown, the nature of a complaint is not a benign act of a concerned citizenry simply exercising its right of grievance and, although a link may be nearly nonexistent, that is, in those incidents where the ultimate decision protected the work from the complaint, complaints as a rule are directly connected to either an actual censorship act or a potential act of censorship. The rationale behind the classification of these four categories, then, supports the definition that is more inclusive through a broader scope. It has also been argued however, that there may be a legitimate reason for censorship that would justify complaints, whether or not citizen challenges are considered censorious. These theories hold that it is inconsequential whether or not a complaint is measured as censorship, but that the distinction should be made between those challenges that are right and those that are made in error.

Walter Berns and Harry Clor are two noted scholars that have presented these ideas. Berns (1970) writes, "Morality cannot be legislated . . . but the law can lend support to the moral dispositions of a people. Tocqueville had this in mind when he warned that the religion which had 'struck its roots deep into a democracy' must be preserved, watched carefully 'as the most precious bequest of aristocratic ages'. The principle can be generalized to apply to all those decent habits that are required for self-government" (1970, 228). Berns and Clor see a danger in a society that promotes the evils of censorship as a threat to democracy. Without censorship, in their minds, the discrimination between art and poor taste becomes blurred. As Burns argues, "the ending of censorship has the effect of establishing the sovereignty of the free mass and commercial market, which is not a market where the arts flourish. With censorship, there is at least one restraint on the commercial republic and it was a moral restraint; the ending of censorship removes the restraint and thereby has the effect of creating or strengthening a public taste for works in which moral questions play no part. But great art deals with moral questions" (1970, 211). To Berns, the promotion of art requires the limitation of that which is in bad taste, and most especially the elimination of obscenity. Most importantly, the people must have the right to complain to protect morality. Clor holds similar views, "For, if there is a public interest in good literature which stimulates the imagination and enlarges the moral horizons of citizens; correspondingly, there is a public interest in the restriction of certain materials which corrupt imagination and contract moral horizons" (1969, 252).

Both Berns and Clor justify censorship challenges on the grounds that obscenity is a substantive evil that must be checked or destroyed. Their treatises have arisen out of and as an attack on Supreme Court decisions, especially the more liberal *Roth* case, that seem to open the way for pornography. However, despite their recognition that censorship is very undemocratic (Clor, 1969) and in the hands of typical censors applied "foolishly and sometimes maliciously" (Berns, 1970, 210), they support the right to challenge materials to protect the moral fiber of society. "To put the case against censorship on the ground that freedom of expression should be granted to everything is to undermine the reason for granting freedom of expression to anything" (Berns, 1970, 210).

There are dangers however, in this approach to the justification of censorship that are only tangentially recognized by those schools of thought that defend censorship. The excesses of the zealots, particularly, in such movements, as well as others, may restrict the precious art so eloquently defended by Berns and Clor, withholding legitimate art that is well within the bounds of good taste as works in poor taste, obscene or objectionable in other ways. Although this is acknowledged in their publications, Berns and Clor are willing to dismiss this problem as a necessary, albeit unfortunate, problem in order to maintain high moral standards. Although there are obvious arguments about who should decide the standards and how lofty they should be, there is plenty of evidence that legitimate art and literature have suffered undue censorship as a result of challenges made by individuals. This research details a substantial number of complaints that were not based on distinctions between art and poor taste or even obscenity and did not involve commercial or mass-market producers of pornography or overtly sexual materials. Contrary to Bern's contention that the conflict over censorship has moved from a distinction between art and trash to one that is a distinction between that which is "utterly" worthless and that which is not "utterly" worthless, the battle is over creative work that is fully legitimate and not obscene but with language or ideas that offend the viewpoints or personal standards of an individual or group. These works are far from the adult bookstore genre of materials or even the soft-core pornography found in many convenience stores. Rather, the complaints vary widely from objections to mild profanity like "damn" or "hell", which is often labeled obscene, to reasons not even closely related to obscenity, such as objectionable criticism of school or governmental authority.

The "chilling effect" that can be caused by suppressive activity, even when employed for what may seem to be proper objections to obscenity or pornography, has the potential for spilling over into works that are acceptable and even to what Berns would view as great art. More importantly, this research and many others, show that most censorship activity is not against hard-core pornography, but legitimate art, literature, and other mediums for expression. This increases the potential impact of the chilling effect on nonobscene works. David K. Berninghausen warns that "censorship is contagious--that it tends to spread from one kind of literature to others" (1975, 6). The problem with discounting any type of complaint or challenge, even one of the first category, is the negative impact it or its accumulative effect may have on the creation, acquisition, or dissemination of other similar works. Since *Catcher in the Rye* is known to be one of the books most consistently censored over the years, would a book about a similar youth's ethical dilemmas be readily created by another author or accepted by another publisher? It is even more likely that a library or school would hesitate, if not outright refuse, to purchase such a title were it to be created.

Therefore, the measurement of complaints must factor in each type or category of complaint to conduct a thorough research. A broader definition, as described by this chapter, will eliminate semantical distinctions between conflicting ideologies, whimsical practices, and the reluctance to properly label a complaint or challenge as censorship. What must be understood, however, is that for this research, the intent of measuring complaints is not to label any one challenge, per se, as evil or to pass judgment on it. Censorship as a phenomena is considered wrong, in general, and the intent of the study is to provide for a greater understanding in order to enhance intellectual freedom through a statistical analysis of the total effect of complaints. However, the fact that any given complaint or challenge may have been fully justified is not within the scope of this study. Only the measurement of such complaints and their characteristics fits within the confines of the design of this research.

CHOICE OF METHOD

The collection and analysis of data on the quantity and properties of censorship incidents has historically been accomplished in one of two forms: the use of surveys and an analysis of reporting sources. The anecdotal record, narrative accounts of specific incidents, may accomplish a goal of gauging the climate or level of censorship if enough accounts are examined and analyzed. The survey method involves the creation of a data- gathering survey or set of surveys. These instruments collect information directly from the point of censorship, generally local institutions, especially schools and libraries, by gathering reported data from individuals directly connected with those institutions. These are usually teachers, librarians, and administrators at the point of censorship as well as other professionals, but they can also be students, parents, and local citizens.

Surveys have a number of advantages over nonscientific techniques. They can be designed so that scientific methods can reduce nonobjective factors as much as possible. A primary difficulty with any kind of inquiry is the introduction of bias into the process. An essential purpose of the scientific method is to make fair and objective statements about an entire phenomena, and especially in research where a conclusion must be made without the benefit of obtaining all of the relevant facts or data, because they are either unobtainable or cannot be gathered in an efficient and effective manner. Bias is a factor or group of factors that thwart the ability of a study to produce useful conclusions about the subject under examination because they are not representative of the phenomena, either in whole or in part. The scientific method, however, recognizes this problem more so than the anecdotal record and is more capable of reducing or eliminating it.

As an example, suppose a study on the acceptability of legal abortions is prepared. A researcher could choose to gather a large number of stories from individuals who have had abortions or who want to express an opinion on the topic. Another method would be a survey that could be designed with or without proper scientific criteria. If this hypothetical survey is asked of only one person, even if that person were selected randomly, the conclusions reached by this response would only reflect that one opinion. A collection of surveys without a scientific design is, then, similar to a collection of anecdotes. A large number of responses could be realized, but the results may not provide valid conclusions if bias has been introduced in any way.

This does not suggest that the opinion of one person surveyed, or that found in several anecdotes, is valueless. Such individual responses and accounts have been known to have an impact in a variety of ways. For example, Nat Hentoff penned a moving account of the censorship of an article written by Priscilla Marco, a student staff member of the Long Island City High School newspaper, *The Skyline* (Hentoff 1988). It is clear, as well as heartening, from the reading of this eloquently reported incident that Priscilla Marco made a significant impact on her high school principal, the Board of Education, and the Long Island City community. It is also certain that the Hentoff account has and will reach many others beyond Long Island, New York and that it can serve to educate and even energize others about the evils of censorship. This, then, is valuable to society as a whole and to intellectual freedom advocates more specifically because of these attributes.

This story, however, cannot suggest anything about the success other student reporters will have or may have if they follow Priscilla Marco's path. It also cannot be used to generalize about the reaction of high school principals or whether or not such criticisms by a student reporter will result in an adverse action in a similar manner. A survey of one does not allow us to make inferences or predictions about other similar circumstances because it lacks the depth of data, at the very least. It must be noted that the purpose of collecting the anecdotal record is not scientific research, but to raise the consciousness of others about the problem of censorship.

In order to examine the issue of bias further, consider the same survey on abortion gathered from every person in the state of Utah. This would substantially increase the sample or number of responses, to over 1.7 million. Despite the fact that such a large number of people would obviously have a greater variety of opinion than a survey of just one person, bias would exist if any conclusions are to be attempted about a state other than Utah, or about all of the states in the United States, or of people in general, because Utah does not represent these other groups. With a large population practicing the Mormon faith, the results from such a hypothetical survey would tend to reflect a more conservative, Mormon-dominated doctrine on abortion than that of a more liberal state such as Massachusetts, for example.

A scientific design to a research project, such as a scientific survey, has the ability to filter out such biases that may occur during the course of the inquiry or data analysis. Furthermore, surveys can gather a very large amount of useful data and information relatively quickly and with greater efficiency and with lower costs than any attempt to collect a similarly significant number of anecdotes. Along with the ability to make generalizations, these constitute the primary strengths of scientific measures as represented by survey technology.

The other method of collecting and analyzing data on censorship that has been used in the past consists of a statistical compilation of information from incident reports already gathered by some other reporting source. This method can make it easier and cheaper to gather a large bank of data on reported censorship cases than the survey or anecdotal methods. However, a primary drawback of this methodology is the lack of control over how the data was initially collected. In other words, bias is a factor in this measurement technique because the original decision to include or exclude an incident is not based on scientific selection, but rather for reasons more germane to the purpose of such reporting sources.

Because this method stresses the use of data that is already gathered, there may be an advantage in having a large amount of information available in one easily accessible source. However, although a large sample size is considered a useful means of reducing the effect of uncontrolled variables, the body of data collected by this methodology does not meet the criteria for a sample. For example, incidents that are not reported are not accounted for in any way, and it appears that these reports make up a substantial number of the total amount of censored materials. It has been widely noted in intellectual freedom literature that only from 4% to 20% of censorship reports have been included in general media outlets. A complaint may have been filed and even settled, but never sent to the local newspaper or media. This may be due to a principal actor in the case intentionally withholding information about the censorship attempt or because no need for reporting the incident was assumed.

Another source of bias in this research technique comes from how the reporting of the cases is initiated. Among most periodicals on censorship, newspapers are usually the form for verifying cases. Most newspaper reports of individual challenges come from either an individual familiar with what is happening or from a reporter's inquiry into institutional matters. The decision to include the story on the incident is made by the newspaper staff based on a judgment as to its newsworthiness, or whether the person initiating the report to the paper (advocate, censor, or reporter), may consider it so. Bias in this decision-making process can occur. However, irrespective of the issue of unreported incidents, newspapers do make a useful source of data on censorship challenges. News reporting requires that news stories be as current as possible and this leaves less room for afterthoughts that may bias the report, for example.

Furthermore, most organs of intellectual freedom advocacy groups that compile a record of censorship incidents rely on newspaper accounts. Bias in what is compiled exists with this methodology because of the difficulties in accessing newspapers from around the nation. Censorship incidents are purely a local matter. The few newspapers that have a national readership record very few local incidents, except those that have received some prominence in the national media as a whole or those of significance to the local constitutiencies they serve, i.e. the *New York Times* coverage of New York City and environs. Papers such as the *New York Times* and the *Washington Post* do not report on a censorship incident in Beeville, Texas, but the *Beeville Bee-Picayune* will because it has local significance to that community. Therefore, to eliminate bias through thoroughness becomes nearly impossible because of the shear number of newspapers to track for censorship accounts. Indexes exist for the *New York Times* and other prominent national newspapers, but not small presses or even large local papers, making access to the full record extremely difficult.

Advocacy organizations also rely on individuals in the field to pass on reports of censorship directly to a national or state/regional office. This is considered to be a form of "self-selection," which is a bias in scientific research. In this design issue, inferences about the total population are hard to make because self-selection does not allow for a measurement of the data as it naturally occurs. It is assumed that individuals who take the time and effort to ensure that the incident is reported have a vested interest in others knowing that the censorship occurred. Furthermore, their personal tastes or biases could fail to send in data as important or even more so than what was actually sent.

However, the purpose of this research is not to make a correlation between two or more variables or to make scientific inferences about censorship. In choosing the methodology for this study, the pitfalls of the two choices were weighed for determining the viability of conducting this research. Although the survey technique possesses many superior qualities for scientific objectivity, it presents too many difficulties in accomplishing the intended goal of measuring complaints. The cost in monetary terms and time constraints were deemed too prohibitive. The analysis of reporting sources proved to be a better option because the data already existed and could be easily gathered. Furthermore, similar studies have been done in the past with which comparisons could be made. The biases inherent in this method are understood to be a given. Since these organizations have a large national membership or hold a prominence in national intellectual freedom affairs, they have a tendency to draw a substantial number of reports that produce a national scope. This body of data is large and, along with the fact that the coverage of reported cases is of a national perspective, it makes this technique a viable one despite the inherent problems in filtering bias. Although this research does not purport to be a design that meets the criteria for purely scientific study, it does have the quality of evaluative, quasi-design research. For the intended outcomes of this project, such a design serves these well.

THE FOUR REPORTING SOURCES

To discover information about any one censorship incident, a newspaper serving the geographic area where the challenge occurred is an excellent source. The depth of detail is better and more current than other reporting sources, some of which merely digest the local paper's account. For the compilation and analysis of censorship cases in their entirety, however, a source that gathers a record of incidents from a variety of reporting mechanisms is better. This can be accomplished, at least to some degree, by examining a newspaper index, especially one such as *The National Newspaper Index*, but to obtain the depth in detail sometimes required by analysis, another step beyond a list of information from the index is needed. The actual source cited in the index has to be examined to gain more knowledge about who the complainant is, what reason was given and the final outcome, and this is extremely time-consuming.

Of all the other sources that record or compile censorship incidents, four periodicals have been found that include several reports in each issue. Each of the four are published by an intellectual freedom advocacy group and each is the result of data gathering from a variety of sources, primarily newspapers, newsletters, and journals of other organizations and reports made directly to a national or state/regional office. Although the four titles may have a different scope and purpose, serve a different clientele, and vary in size or number of incidents reported, they are all journals designed to combat censorship in some way.

L. B. Woods' 1979 book, *A Decade of Censorship in America* utilized one of these, *The Newsletter on Intellectual Freedom*. It is the oldest of the four mentioned, and as stated earlier, primarily serves the library profession. After the Reagan victory in 1980, a reinvigorated right-wing political movement was spawned. Norman Lear, the producer of the hit television program *All in the Family*, formed People for the American Way to counter this conservative wave of political pressure pushing for a more restrictive environment. This organization publishes the annual *Attacks on the Freedom to Learn*. It was begun in 1982 as a sampling of censorship incidents in educational institutions. The National Coalition Against Censorship was formed in 1974 as a cooperative effort of several professional associations concerned about intellectual freedom, especially the Association of American Publishers, the American Library Association (ALA), and the American Civil Liberties Union, with the purpose of combatting censorship through information campaigns and various other educational efforts. They publish a quarterly newsletter, *Censorship News* begun in 1974, that includes reports of censorship incidents. Lastly, the Student Press Law Center, a student journalism advocacy organization, also begun in 1974, publishes *The Student Press Law Center Report* three times annually. In addition to news articles on student reporters' rights, legislation affecting the student press and court cases relevant to student journalism, the *SPLC Report* publishes censorship incidents involving any form of student journalism, particularly newspapers, yearbooks, literary and art magazines, as well as student broadcasting, both television and radio, with an occasional report on textbook or other accounts of censorship of materials used in the schools or colleges.

These four periodicals have been chosen because all four record numerous censorship incidents in each issue and gather information in a similar, systematic way, primarily through tracking reports in newspapers and journals. In addition to the amount of data they provide, a national coverage and scope is provided by their method of data collection. Newspapers from around the nation are culled for relevant news stories and a large and committed membership adds to the body of data with unsolicited reports that may not have reached the papers examined for the data gathering.

The Newsletter on Intellectual Freedom is an excellent source for reading about censorship incidents. It does not limit itself to any one type of institution or constituency. Educational institutions, libraries of any type, museums, retail outlets, governmental agencies, even public street corner activities are covered. It also does not limit itself to any one form of expression or medium. Reports on books, periodicals, speeches, films, plays, art, museum exhibits, advertisements, among many others, are given equal reportage. Six issues a year provide brief synopses of each incident listed. Although these reports are not in-depth news coverage, a surprising wealth of information is provided, including who the major players in the situation are, what the complaint targeted and for what reason, what action, if any, was taken at the time of the report and any relevant comments by the principal actors, in addition to incidental information such as date and locale. Furthermore, and of great importance to this study, follow up reports are included that reference past issues and previously recorded incidents. This was useful in this study to determine the final disposition of a given case.

The Newsletter has two sections expressly devoted to the recording of censorship cases, "Censorship Dateline" and "Success Stories. In addition, two sections provide reports and analyses of legislation and court cases, entitled "Is It Legal" and "From the Bench." Although these are often news items or analysis of current legal events, specific instances are occasionally included. *The Newsletter* also reports on issues of religious freedom, freedom of the press, reporters' rights, and difficulties in the protection of the right to assembly. As these issues are not directly germane to censorship, these accounts were not gathered or analyzed. The content and format of *The Newsletter on Intellectual Freedom* is sufficient to rival any scholarly publication on this topic for its impact and usefulness, and also includes features similar to these publications, including an extensive bibliography of current sources on censorship or intellectual freedom, significant opinions, reports and surveys, conference papers, intellectual freedom award winners and book reviews.

The Attacks on the Freedom to Learn is published once a year. Its purpose is to report on the state of censorship in the nation's educational institutions for that given time period. The first section is a substantial essay describing trends and issues that occurred. The second, and more relevant portion for this study, is a state-by-state report of censorship incidents. This publication has some notable limitations for the purpose of this work. No attempt to be comprehensive is made, but the publisher makes it clear that the cases are a representative sample of the incidents reported to their office and validated by staff members. People for the American Way takes extra steps to document and verify each case to ensure that it has been reported in a standard news source. Also, the cases are those that have occurred at educational institutions. Other censorship situations, such as museums, books stores, or public forums are generally not included.

Each incident recorded includes a brief synopsis of the details in a list format. Each entry has an explanation of what was challenged and includes the title, if one exists, and a brief description of the challenge, who the initiator of the challenge was, and the end result. The source that was used to verify the case is also reproduced. The annual concludes with an alphabetical list of the titles censored and indicates the number of challenges, if more than one occurred.

Censorship News, which is published four times a year, has been included in this research because it is the reporting organ of a major intellectual freedom advocacy organization, the National Coalition Against Censorship. *Censorship News* is produced in newsletter format. Each page contains at least one report or essay on a current issue on this topic or a specific incident. Information on each case as well as the number of incidents reported varies from issue to issue.

because of the strength of arguments made in each essay.

The scope of the first three periodical titles mentioned above covers a general range of censorship cases, although in some instances the reportage is limited. The final periodical utilized in this research has a more narrow focus, but each issue contains a substantial number of very detailed reports. *The Student Press Law Center Report* is published three times annually. A significant number of articles report, in-depth, censorship incidents that were perpetrated against a student-produced medium, primarily newspapers, yearbooks, and literary and art magazines, but most any form of student-created publication. Other works mentioned have included pamphlets, class newsletters, or projects; posters and advertisements, and student radio and television broadcasts.

The SPLC Report is a news-like magazine. Each issue contains several sections, one of which is devoted to reporting censorship cases. Other sections, particularly those on advisers, libel cases, and court cases, often report on censorship incidents as well. Each of the reports is written and laid out in newspaper style and the information provided is quite detailed, although some of the articles do not include specific dates.

This research could have utilized other works for the purpose of data collection. The following are some of the more relevant titles and an explanation as to why they were not used. *The Index on Censorship* is a publication of an international intellectual freedom advocacy organization, Article 19. It includes reports on censorship incidents in a format similar to that of *The Newsletter on Intellectual Freedom*, but its primary emphasis is on international aspects and cases. *The World Report on Censorship* is also published by Article 19 and reports cases from around the world. Article 19 is named for the section of the United Nations charter that calls for and promotes intellectual freedom in its member nations. *News Media and the Law* is a publication of the Reporters' Committee for Freedom of the Press. It is comparable to *The Student Press Law Center Report* but has not been included because of limitations in its coverage of censorship incidents and in order to conduct a more efficient research project for this work. Furthermore, two titles worth mentioning to anyone interested in intellectual freedom are *Civil Liberties*, the journal of the American Civil Liberties Union, and *The Harvard Civil Rights-Civil Liberties Law Review*. Both are excellent sources for analysis of current events and trends in intellectual freedom, however, their format consists of weighty essays, not the incidental reports needed for this research.

THE DATA COLLECTION

Chapter 1 outlined ten questions this research seeks to answer for the decade 1981-1990. To discover these answers, data from nine distinct categories were recorded from each relevant censorship incident included in the four intellectual recorded from each relevant censorship incident included in the four intellectual freedom journals detailed above. Eight of these categories are similar to those in *A Decade of Censorship in America*. A ninth item, intellectual freedom advocates, was added because it is believed to be as important to measure those groups or individuals willing to combat censorship as it is those groups or individuals who would challenge a form of expression. For each case reported, an index card was prepared with the following information:

1. THE TITLE:

2. THE TYPE OF MATERIAL OR EXPRESSIVE FORM:

3. THE YEAR OF THE COMPLAINT:

4. THE LOCATION OF THE CHALLENGE:

5. THE INSTITUTION WHERE THE CHALLENGE OCCURRED:

6. THE COMPLAINANT, OR THE INDIVIDUAL OR GROUP THAT FILED A CHAL-LENGE OR IN SOME WAY MADE A COMPLAINT:

7. THE REASON STATED WHY THE FORM OF EXPRESSION WAS OBJECTION-ABLE:

8. THE RESULT OR ACTION TAKEN:

9. THE ADVOCATES:

The complete title was recorded for all items listing a formal title, including the titles of paintings and other forms of expression not similar to the book form. If no title was reported, a brief, title-like description was composed. The author's name is included on the card, where available, although this information is not compiled for this study. It is believed that author information may be useful at a later date.

Past research and reports have shown that censorship is not limited to the traditional book form. Any form of expression, be it art, films, plays, radio and television broadcasts, or even public speeches, are subject to challenges. New forms of expression, such as t-shirts, bumper stickers, and vanity license plates have experienced growing censorship objections. A list of nineteen types of expression, in various formats, were recognized and recorded. Similar types of formats have been grouped together, for example, any type of exhibit including those found in art museums, science centers, or in schools and businesses, because their format characteristics are not substantially different from one another. No distinction was noted for periodicals, which included journals, magazines, and newsletters. Student newspapers were treated as a separate category from all other student publications and included student alternative or underground presses. Preliminary data indicated that student produced papers were censored in much larger numbers than any other type of student publication. Yearbooks, literary and art magazines, and other publications, such as newsletters and pamphlets were included in one format category except for the analysis of the *SPLC* report.

In measuring the location of censorship incidents, the state where the incident occurred was recorded. Some of the sources include the city or local jurisdiction where the complaint was made and some do not, therefore, only the state was entered into the data program. This research design also eliminated any report from a foreign nation, including Canada. There are reasons for an American focus. The First Amendment rights enjoyed by American citizens are unique and have decidedly different character than intellectual freedom rights of the peoples of other nations. Furthermore, the analysis of the data is less diffuse.

Institutions are generally thought of as physical facilities, such as schools, libraries and museums. However, this work defines an institution as any organization, place, or industry responsible for the production, distribution, or control of the use of the item subjected to a censorship challenge. In most cases, the censorship attempt occurred within a recognizable institution, such as a library or school. However, over twenty-eight distinct categories of institutions were identified in this study. A number of items, particularly newspapers, books, and periodicals, experienced a form of prior restraint before the item was ever produced. In this situation, the publishing industry responsible for the work was considered the institution for this purpose. In other cases, the distributor was prevented from distributing the item or refused to do so, therefore, retail business, and other types of distributors were recorded as the institution.

As with the format of expression, some categories with institutions of a like nature were grouped together, such as museums categorized with science centers or other exhibits. In the case of educational institutions, a distinction is made by level of education--elementary, junior high or middle school, high school and college, university, or community college--and whether the challenge occurred against a school-owned or -used material or material of a specific level of a library within the school. In other words, each type of library-- elementary, junior high or middle school, and senior high--is considered a separate institution from the school itself, except for universities, colleges, and community colleges. Very few reported incidents of censorship have been found for academic libraries, so these have been included in the university, college, or community college category rather than in a separate category of their own.

For the purpose of this study, a complaint to a school about a textbook or other material used in the classroom, a student publication, a film or play shown or performed in the school, or for a school audience and any other activity not connected with the library or its collection is considered a separate entry under a "school" category and any incident that concerned a library resource or activity in the library is recorded in the appropriate level library category. A need for more generic categories is also required for those reports that made no distinction of level or sub-type of institution. "School Library" is used for any incident occurring in a library not designated as a separate level. "School" or "School District" is used when no distinction is made as to the level of school. Furthermore, a distinction is made between a theater used to screen a film or live-stage play or production, and stage performances not linked to a performance of a written work. These include such activities as stage or nightclub dancers, striptease dancers, stand-up comedians, and beauty pageants.

Utilizing the definition of complaint as described in this chapter, over sixty-four distinct categories of complaints were identified. As with other data points, similar types were grouped together in one category. For example, no distinction was made concerning the type of minister, priest, or rabbi. All religious authorities are included in one category. All professionals in a community, such as doctors, lawyers, dentists, psychologists, or pharmacists, are grouped together. Where an organization held some national prominence, such as the Moral Majority, a separate category has been included. If the name of the group could be found in a standard reference book, it was considered to be within this definition of national prominence. If not, or if the article indicated the group existed only in that locale, this entry has been entered into a generic category "Other organization." Personal names have been avoided, except with some nationally known public figures, such as the Rev. Jerry Falwell, founder and president of the Liberty Federation, formerly the Moral Majority. If more than one type of complainant was noted in the article, each appropriate category was marked on the data cards.

Over fifty-four distinct reasons why an item might be a target for censorship are found in this inquiry. Often, more than one reason was given, and these multiples are recorded for each case. Again, as with other categories, a grouping of similar reasons was made. For example, pornographic and obscene are seen as synonymous and included in one category. However, in many instances, the complainant did not view the item as obscene or pornographic, but still objected to some form of sexual content or explicitness. A separate category was created for this reason. Profanity and vulgar language are likewise grouped together, but use of the term "nigger," although profane in the eyes of many, was included in the "Racist" category because of the problems that word causes with the various races. In several incidents, there was an official reason stated that appeared to cloak a content-based reason for the complaint. For example, some cases reported that the school principal censored a student publication because it was poorly written or because of "poor grammar" but the report indicated that the highly critical nature of the article, often directly attacking the principal, played a substantial role in the censorship. Both reasons were recorded in these instances. Some categories grouped together reasons that seem to be dichotomous in nature, but are viewed as a flip-sided approach to the same problem. For example, some individuals complained that a book promoted Darwin's theory of evolution while others objected to a book that did not promote a creation science approach to the creation of the world. Every attempt has been made to track through subsequent reports to determine the final outcome for each case. The last known result is the one recorded for data analysis. Over forty-three distinct categories of results were ascertained. The literature of intellectual freedom, especially those addressed to librarians, stresses the importance of review committees. However, review committees generally are not the final word concerning a censorship incident. Several categories exist that record the possible decisions a review committee can take. If the last known result is a review committee action, one of these categories has been marked. If the last known result indicates that a governing board accepted a review committee decision, a category reflecting this result is marked. Many of the news reports have indicated only that a complaint was made. If subsequent tracking of the incident did not discover any other result, only the category for "complaint filed" was recorded. This does not mean that no other result occurred, but only that this research found no other outcome.

The measurement of the advocates for a censored item is a new approach to a statistical study of censorship. Any person or group that took a positive action toward defending the expressive rights of others or who in some way confronted a complainant in a censorship challenge is considered to be an advocate for the purpose of this study. If a person or a spokesperson for a group is quoted in a way that appears to have been elicited merely for an opinion on the topic, then an advocate category was not recorded in these instances. A review committee or governing board performing their mandate to review and pass judgment on the worthiness of an item, even if their ultimate decision ended in support of the item censored, is not considered in an advocate role. Similarly, librarians in defense of their own collection or teachers at the center of a textbook or instructional program complaint in their own classroom are not considered advocates. Such individuals, as part of their normal duties, are seen as required to defend, at least in some small way, the materials they keep or use because of the professional codes they subscribe to, such as the "Library Bill of Rights." Advocates are seen as those individuals or groups that do not have to place themselves in harms way in defense of expression. Although teachers and librarians at the center of a censorship controversy have often been vehement advocates for a material being challenged, and can face loss of their position or other dangerous situations, they are seen as having a vested interest in the defense of the item.

Once the data gathering on the cards was complete, a spreadsheet file was created to store and manipulate the data. One file was created for each of the four sets of data from the four journals analyzed. These computer files were used to tally the statistics for use in the analysis and to sort like data by categories or characteristics. These final results were used to draw conclusions about the climate of censorship during the 1980s and to answer the ten questions posed in the beginning of the research. This analysis, including supporting data, can be found in the succeeding chapters. The data permits a comparison of coverage of each of the four reporting sources. Comparisons are also made to the results generated by L. B. Woods (1979) for the decade 1966-1975 and to the information provided in the appendices of Lee Burress' *The Battle of the Books* (1989).

BENCHMARKING

In addition to the compilation and comparison of the data gathered for the 1980s, the results of this study have been compared to three independent indexes and compilations of censored materials. The intent of this process is to utilize each source as a "benchmark" for the data gained in this survey. This kind of comparison can show how accurate the answers to the research questions are compared with other established research or with other sources listing censorship incidents.

Both L. B. Woods' *A Decade of Censorship in America* (1979) and Lee Burress' *Battle of the Books* (1989) are research projects of long standing. The results each book has reported have been an integral part of intellectual freedom studies and articles for the past decade and more. Their research has determined a set of statistics that show what titles are most often challenged, for what reasons, and by what individuals or parties. These statistics are grounded in a well-developed research technique, and as a result have won prominence in the literature of intellectual freedom. The results of this work are compared to test where any differential in the data may exist and to indicate any similarities. This was accomplished by matching the list of titles in each publication in rank order by total number of censorship attempts, and other relevant matchings, including institutions, complainants, and reasons.

Furthermore, as an additional test of the data, the results were benchmarked against the index for the same years, 1981-1990, of the *National Newspaper Index*. An in-depth comparison of the final statistics with this index has not been attempted (primarily due to limited resources). However, the purpose of this comparison is to determine if there are any significant differences in the titles reported by the two different sources, that is *The National Newspaper Index* and the accumulated total of the four periodicals studied in this text. This comparison is a further check on how accurate the results of the study may be, and will be reported in subsequent publications.

4   Data Analysis

We have given the 1980s many different names over the years--the Me Decade, the Era of the Hostile Takeover, and the Age of AIDS. Whatever nametag we put on it, it has often been thought of as a time when Americans moved toward, or returned to, more conservative values than were popular in the 1960s and 1970s. President Reagan's mustering of a Neoconservative alliance signaled the beginning of new political era and marked the end of over two decades of progressive domestic social policy (even during the Nixon years). "Family Values" became a popular rallying cry of figures both within the Reagan administration and in public offices nationwide.

Civil libertarians early in the decade feared that this conservative mobilization would bring with it a decline in respect throughout the body politic for individual freedoms. If one considers censorship attempts as a barometer of such a disregard for individual rights, then a mere glance at the number of incidents reported in the *Newsletter on Intellectual Freedom* for the 1980s bears this fear out (see Table 4.1). From its high point of 365 in 1981 (the year of Reagan's inauguration) the number of incidents reported in the *NIF* shows a slow dissipation of national interest in censorship over the decade, with a precipitous drop taking place throughout the first years of the Bush presidency. A linear regression analysis for 1981-1989 shows a downward tendency throughout those years (r = -0.772). Because this study ends with the year 1990, no measure is available as to whether the controversy that engulfed Robert Mapplethorpe and the National Endowment for the Arts (NEA) had any significant affect in general on our desire to censor.

The decline in the number of incidents over the decade suggests, although it cannot be numerically demonstrated, that under the charismatic leadership of Reagan, many Americans were spurred on to acts of civil indignity, and that this charisma gradually faded over time, almost to the point of disappearing under Bush's watch. This is interesting, because the Bush rhetoric certainly maintained the emphasis on "family values," but perhaps the call for a "kinder, gentler

Table 4.1 Total Number of Censorship Attempts per Year with Change in Number and Percentage over the Previous Year for *NIF*

YEAR	NIF	NIF CHANGE	NIF % CHANGE	CN	ATFL	SPLC
1981	365	-	-	5	0	7
1982	259	-106	-29.04	0	17	9
1983	233	-26	-10.03	6	33	12
1984	290	+57	+24.46	5	36	23
1985	232	-58	-20.00	8	25	24
1986	230	-2	-0.86	5	33	29
1987	270	+42	+18.42	4	56	28
1988	167	-103	-38.15	1	34	33
1989	77	-90	-53.89	3	62	37
1990	51	-26	-33.77	3	48	31

Sources: *Newsletter on Intellectual Freedom* (1981-1990); *Censorship News* (1981-1990); *Attacks on the Freedom to Learn* (1982-1990); *Student Press Law Center Report* (1981-1990); *Decade of Censorship in America* by L. B. Woods (1979).

nation" produced a less censorious one also. The dissolution of Reagan's conservative coalition must also be considered; Bush never could convincingly gather the forces of the far right and thus was not a factor in the mobilization of the conservative agenda. His defeat in the 1992 election was the final demonstration of this inability.

The other censorship reporting sources that have been analyzed here all came into existence much later than *NIF*, one as a result of identifying the Reagan leadership as a "threat" to intellectual freedom, thus they are less useful for comparative studies over several years. Each source also reports on far fewer incidents than *NIF*, making significant figures difficult to obtain. Figure 4.1 demonstrates this disparity in totals for all four sources throughout the decade. Of these, *Attacks on the Freedom to Learn* reports the greatest number of incidents, but actually shows peak activity later in the decade. *Censorship News* shows a similar late-decade peak. It is probably safe to say that these higher numbers later in the 1980s reflect a change in their procedures for reporting incidents and perhaps an increase in their vigilance of intellectual freedom issues. *ATFL* continues to report each year that censorship is increasing, but their publication only carries detailed stories on a select number of these incidents.

CENSORSHIP: WHAT ARE THE TARGETS?

This study identified 2,174 censorship attempts reported in the *Newsletter on Intellectual Freedom* during the decade 1981-1990. During this same decade,

Figure 4.1 Number of Challenges According to Year

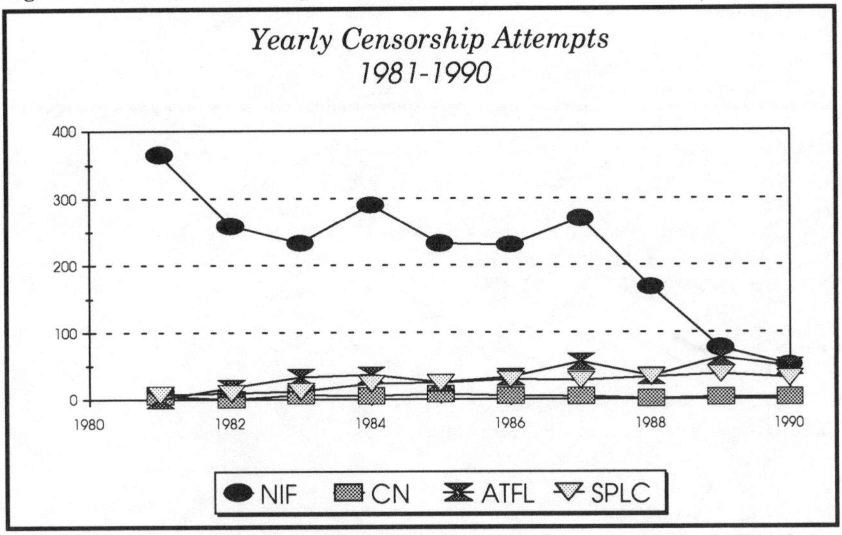

Yearly Censorship Attempts
1981-1990

● NIF   ▦ CN   ▪ ATFL   ▽ SPLC

Sources: Newsletter on Intellectual Freedom; Censorship News; Attacks on the Freedom to Learn; Student Press Law Center Report.

the *Attacks on the Freedom to Learn* reported 344 attempts, *Censorship News* included 41 incidents in their articles, and the *Student Press Law Center Report* 234 attempts. These statistics do not represent isolated situations nor completely unique objects of censorship in all cases. Significant numbers of challenges have been noted against many known and not so known expressive works. In 1978, L. B. Woods reported the greatest number of challenges to one item during the decade 1966-1975, as reported in ALA's *Newsletter on Intellectual Freedom*, to be forty-one, against *Catcher in the Rye*. The *Newsletter* for this more current decade reports a similar frequency, forty-seven attempts against *Playboy* magazine (see Table 4.2). Of the 2,174 cases in the *NIF*, 1,258 are a title or item that appears only once. Another 129 works have only two challenges recorded during this decade. Although two censorship attempts may be considered substantial in some corners, three or more challenges is considered to be significant by this research because it creates a more manageable list and because it permits a better comparison with the work of L. B. Woods who also analyzed challenges of materials with three or more attempts. The remaining 630 cases represent the most censored materials of the 1980s (see Table 4.2). There are 106 unique titles amongst these cases, which yields an average of 5.94 challenges per item. Twenty-eight works are above this average, of which eighteen are books, six are magazines, one each of a game, comic strip, textbook, and film.

Of the other three reporting sources, only the *Attacks on the Freedom to Learn*

Table 4.2 Significant Titles (Those with Three or More Censorship Attempts) According to Format

TITLE/ SOURCE	NIF	ATFL	CN	SPLC
BOOKS				
Deenie	18	3	2	
Forever	17		4	
Then Again, Maybe I Won't	17	3	3	
Adventures of Huckleberry Finn	16			
Of Mice and Men	15	4		
Show Me!	15			
Go Ask Alice	13	5		
Blubber	11	4		
Catcher in the Rye	11	8		
Are You There, God? It's Me, Margaret	10			
Changing Bodies, Changing Lives	9			
The Chocolate War	9	5		
Our Bodies, Ourselves	9			
The Color Purple	8			
A Light in the Attic	8			
Slaughterhouse Five	8			
Flowers For Algernon	6			
To Kill a Mockingbird	6			
Brave New World	5			
Cujo	5	5		
A Day No Pigs Would Die	5			
Vision Quest	5			
Where the Sidewalk Ends	5			
Bloodline	4			
Grapes of Wrath	4			
I Know Why the Caged Bird Sings	4	3		
It's Not the End of the World	4			
It's OK if You Don't Love Me	4			
Lord of the Flies	4			
Ordinary People	4			
Run, Shelley, Run!	4			
Salem's Lot	4			
The Shining	4			
Where Do Babies Come From?	4			
Boys and Sex	3			
Christine	3			
Firestarter	3			
Great Gatsby	3			
Great Gilly Hopkins	3			
Grendel	3			
Hard Feelings	3			
Headman	3			
In the Spirit of Crazy Horse	3			

Table 4.2 (continued)

Title/Source	NIF	ATFL	CN	SPLC
Joy of Sex	3			
Last Mission	3			
Manchild in the Promised Land	3			
Once is Not Enough	3			
One Flew Over the Cuckoo's Nest	3			
Our Land, Our Time	3			
Petals on the Wind	3			
A Separate Peace	3			
Sisters Impossible	3			
Starring Sally J. Freedman as Herself	3			
Valley of the Horses	3			
Witches	3			
Working	3			
Curses, Hexes and Spells		4		
Halloween ABC		3		
I Am the Cheese		3		
Servants of the Devil		3		

COMIC BOOKS AND COMICS

Doonesbury	10			
Dondi	3			

FILMS

Last Temptation of Christ	9			
Deep Throat	5			
Hail Mary	5			
Romeo and Juliet	5	3		
Debbie Does Dallas	4			
Ordinary People	4			
The Shining	4			
Birth of a Nation	3			
La Cage Aux Folles	3			
Last Tango in Paris	3			
Caligula	3			
Spermbusters	3			

GAMES

Dungeons & Dragons	10			

MAGAZINES

Playboy	47			
Penthouse	25			
Hustler	10			
Playgirl	10			
Sports Illustrated	8	3		
Oui	6			
Ms.	5			
Chic	4			

Table 4.2 (continued)

Title/Source	NIF	CN	ATFL	SPLC
High Society	4			
Issues and Answers	4			4
Rolling Stone	4			
Life	3			
National Lampoon	3			
Newsweek	3			
Penthouse Forum	3			
PLAYS				
Sister Mary Ignasius Explains It All To You	6			
Oh! Calcutta	4			
Pippin	3			
STUDENT NEWSPAPER				
Salem State College Log	3			
TEXTBOOKS				
Married and Single Life	6			
Finding My Way	5			
Impressions Textbook Series	5	6		
Romeo and Juliet	5			
Biology	4			
Let's Talk About Health	4			
Modern Human Sexuality	4			
Adolescents Today	3			
Family Matters	3			
Humanities: Cultural Roots and Continuities	3			
Married Life	3			
Parenting and Children	3			
Person to Person	3			
Sociology	3			
Street Law	3			
Understanding Health	3			
Understanding Your Sexuality	3			

Sources: Newsletter on Intellectual Freedom (1981-1990); *Attacks on the Freedom to Learn* (1982-1990); *Censorship News* (1981-1990); *Student Press Law Center Report* (1981-1990).

has reported such significant challenges to any expressive works (see Table 4.2). *Censorship News* has only recorded more than one censorship attempt for two books: *Deenie* and *Then Again, Maybe I Won't*, both by Judy Blume. The *Student Press Law Center Report* shows only nine of 224 unique items with two or more censorship attempts, with a maximum of four recorded attempts against one title. The *ATFL*, however, has found thirty-three unique titles, of 279, with two or more censorship attempts from 1982 through 1990. However, only sixteen of these compare in magnitude to the levels of censorship found in the *Newsletter on Intellectual Freedom* with three or more challenges, fourteen of which are books, while one is a film (*Romeo and Juliet*) and one is a magazine (*Sports Illustrated*'s swimsuit issue).

During the years 1981 through 1990, *Playboy* magazine has been the most censored material of all reported cases of censorship. Although the total number of individual periodical titles is small compared to challenged books, six titles account for almost one third of all the challenges to those items with an above average frequency of censorship attempts (Table 4.2). Five of these six titles, *Playboy, Penthouse, Hustler, Playgirl*, and *Oui*, are known as softcore pornography, with all but *Playgirl* catering to men's tastes in feature articles and photo subjects. Three other softcore pornographic titles, *Chic, High Society*, and *Penthouse Forum* are among the fifteen magazines with three or more recorded censorship attempts reported in the *NIF*. Only the *Sports Illustrated* swimsuit issue can compare to the magnitude of challenges of any in this genre of periodicals, with eight recorded censorship complaints.

During the Reagan/Bush years, the *Newsletter on Intellectual Freedom* has shown that several books by Judy Blume are the most censored books in the nation. Three titles in particular-- *Deenie, Forever*, and *Then Again, Maybe I Won't* have more challenges reported in the *NIF* than any other book except Mark Twain's *The Adventures of Huckleberry Finn*, which is the third most challenged book (see Table 4.2). Furthermore, five of the ten most censored book titles are written by Judy Blume. In years past, it has often been reported that the most censored book is *Catcher in the Rye*. This data does not support that conclusion for the 1980s. J. D. Salinger's classic has been censored eleven times during the decade, far fewer times than in the 1966-1975 decade and ranks tenth in the list of book titles censored (Table 4.2).

Compared to pulp fiction or to any type of pornography, censorship of classics or critically acclaimed literature has usually been considered unreasonable in most circles. At least a dozen such books have received substantial numbers of complaints, with *Of Mice and Men, Catcher in the Rye, Slaughterhouse Five, Flowers for Algernon, To Kill a Mockingbird*, and *Brave New World* among the most censored books of the 1980s, in addition to Mark Twain's *Adventures of Huckleberry Finn*, as mentioned earlier. More recent books of note have also proven to be highly censored. *Changing Bodies, Changing Lives* and *Our Bodies, Ourselves*, two books on human sexuality, have been the target of the censor nine times each during the decade. Robert Cormier's *The Chocolate War* has also been attacked in a significant way, as well as Alice Walker's *The Color Purple*. Two very popular books of children's poetry by Shel Silverstein, *A Light In the Attic* and *Where the Sidewalk Ends*, are frequent targets, although only *A Light in the Attic* has an above average number of attempts (Table 4.2).

Of the other three sources studied, *The Attacks on the Freedom to Learn* supports the earlier conclusions that *Catcher in the Rye* is the most censored book, although the magnitude of attempts recorded is not as significant as the *Newsletter's* twenty most-censored titles (Table 4.2). The remaining titles on the *ATFL's* list of books with substantial censorship attempts are primarily children's and young adult books. Four of these nine titles for younger audiences are written by Judy Blume. Robert Cormier's *The Chocolate War* as well as *Go Ask Alice* have also been reported by the *ATFL* as serious targets of the censor.

Films and plays do not constitute a large portion of the materials challenged in the 1980s. However, several productions can be found in the data and a few have had a substantial number of challenges. The *Newsletter on Intellectual Freedom* has more useful data and it shows that *The Last Temptation of Christ* was the most censored film of the 1980s (Table 4.2). Pornographic films are more obvious targets and two of these, *Deep Throat* and *Debbie Does Dallas*, have gained enough notoriety to be attacked several times, usually when booked at institutions other than an adult film theater. The Franco Zeffirelli production of *Romeo and Juliet* also has been challenged on five occasions as reported by both the *Newsletter* and the *Attacks on the Freedom to Learn* most often because of concerns over teen suicides. Only three plays meet the criteria for substantial censorship as defined by this study. The satiric *Sister Mary Ignatius Explains It All for You* is the most censored play of this decade. It has been attacked most often by the Catholic League for Religious and Civil Liberties and Catholic state legislators.

Textbook censorship has been viewed as a different form than that of book censorship. Textbooks are purchased as required reading and instruction for school students. Books, however, are often available for people to choose to read on their own, with the possible exception of required reading lists for literature classes. Again, the *Newsletter on Intellectual Freedom* has the most significant data on these materials. The human sexuality text *Married and Single Life* (Table 4.2), published by Bennett Publishing has been challenged the most during the 1980s; however, two other texts, *Finding My Way*, also published by Bennett and the *Impressions* textbook series experienced almost the same number of complaints. Of the seventeen textbooks with three or more attempts to remove them from use in a school, at least eleven are health and human sexuality texts. Of those textbooks reported by the other three sources of this research, none have any significant challenges. However, *Censorship News* also reported the texts *Family Matters*, published by Sterling Publishing, and *Person to Person*, published by National Textbook Co., as censored titles as did the *NIF. Humani-*

ties: Cultural Roots and Continuities, published by D. C. Heath, has recorded attempts in both the *Attacks on the Freedom to Learn* and the *Newsletter on Intellectual Freedom.*

None of the remaining formats identified by this research have any one individual item with substantial number of censorship attacks, with the exception of the game "Dungeons & Dragons," and the comic strip "Doonesbury" (Table 4.2). It is interesting to note that the *Newsletter on Intellectual Freedom* has discovered seventy-nine separate incidents of art censorship and nineteen exhibits that have foregone some form of attempt at suppression (see Appendix). Somewhat more disturbing are the attempts to censor government information. Although there are only eight separate incidents found in the *Newsletter* for this time period, most cases have been initiated by a member of President Reagan's administration.

The censored materials reported in the *Student Press Law Center Report* are almost entirely student publications. Only nine individual items experienced more than one challenge, and only two have been attacked more than twice, a Christian newspaper *Issues and Answers* and the Salem State College student newspaper, *The Log* (Table 4.2). The significant statistics arise from the total number of student newspaper and alternative newspaper titles, rather than from individual titles. During the 1980s, 153 approved student newspapers have been censored in some way and twenty-two alternative newspapers have also been attacked (see Appendix).

CENSORSHIP: WHERE DOES IT OCCUR?

A geographic analysis of censorship is a tempting endeavor, which L. B. Woods has readily undertaken, yet it is not at all clear that there is a significant regional effect on the number of incidents. Certainly, incidents may be stimulated locally by popular issues or vocal public officials, but it becomes difficult to measure how this might affect the total number of events statewide or regionally.

Woods attempted to relate some per capita figures for censorship in each state in his research. Although his numbers are not strictly speaking per capita at all, but simply percentages of the total incidents occurring in each state divided by the percentage of total United States population in that state. One drawback with this method is that he used population figures from one year to determine an index of censorship over a ten-year period. On the other hand, a strictly per capita figure for the states--obtained by averaging the observed incidents per 100,00 population in each year from 1981 through 1989--delivers, in relative terms, the same result as Woods' method (Table 4.3). The two sets of figures for each state show a high degree of correlation ($r = 0.997$). This seems to indicate that the population effect in the number of reported incidents accounted

Table 4.3 Censorship Incidents in the *NIF* with Rankings and Year of Highest Censorship

STATE	INCIDENTS	% OF TOTAL	INDEX	PERCAP	RANK	YEAR
AL	41	1.91	1.17	0.112	24	1981
AK	2	0.09	0.41	0.043	43	1984
AR	26	1.20	0.82	0.076	32	1981
CA	187	8.63	0.72	0.074	36	1984
CO	71	3.27	2.48	0.229	4	1986
CT	24	1.11	0.84	0.079	31	1989
DE	7	0.32	1.19	0.126	23	1981
DC	68	3.14	13.08	1.157	1	1984
FL	161	7.43	1.43	0.157	16	1982
GA	44	2.03	0.78	0.080	34	1987
HI	0				45	
ID	13	0.60	1.50	0.146	15	1981
IL	100	4.61	1.00	0.091	27	1984
IN	27	1.25	0.56	0.053	40	1982
IA	50	2.31	2.06	0.182	9	1987
KS	26	1.20	1.20	0.109	22	1981
KY	30	1.38	1.20	0.090	22	1982
LA	37	1.71	1.00	0.093	27	1985
ME	19	0.88	1.80	0.174	12	1984
MD	52	2.40	1.25	0.125	20	1981
MA	50	2.31	0.95	0.089	28	1983
MI	73	3.37	0.90	0.087	29	1982
MN	59	2.72	1.55	0.144	14	1983
MS	11	0.51	0.50	0.043	41	1984
MO	38	1.75	0.85	0.084	30	1982
MT	16	0.75	2.31	0.218	7	1985
NE	36	1.66	2.63	0.244	3	1987
NV	11	0.51	1.06	0.128	26	1987
NH	13	0.60	1.33	0.151	17	1982
NJ	28	1.28	0.41	0.040	43	1984
NM	17	0.78	1.28	0.78	18	1982
NY	103	4.75	0.66	0.057	37	1982
NC	38	1.75	0.66	0.066	37	1981
ND	10	0.46	1.77	0.164	13	1986
OH	56	2.58	0.56	0.054	40	1983
OK	22	1.01	0.80	0.062	33	1986
OR	45	2.07	1.82	0.181	11	1984
PA	76	3.50	0.73	0.067	35	1985
RI	16	0.70	1.85	0.186	10	1981
SC	11	0.51	0.36	0.037	44	1985
SD	14	0.65	2.32	0.221	6	1983
TN	24	1.11	0.57	0.057	39	1981
TX	67	3.09	0.45	0.045	42	1981
UT	9	0.42	0.61	0.062	38	1981
VT	11	0.51	2.22	0.234	8	1981

Table 4.3 (continued)

STATE	INCIDENTS	%OF TOTAL	INDEX	PERCAP	RANK	YEAR
VA	67	3.09	1.24	0.113	21	1983
WA	78	3.60	1.85	0.190	10	1987
WV	18	0.83	1.15	0.094	25	1989
WI	104	4.80	2.44	0.240	5	1986
WY	36	1.66	9.22	0.765	2	1984

Source: Newsletter on Intellectual Freedom (1981-1990).

for by either method.

By using either an index such as Woods' or the per capita method, the Midwest is generally the most censorious region (Table 4.4), and has a number of the most censorious states within its boundaries. Although the District of Columbia has the highest index of censorship in the country, Wisconsin, South Dakota, and Iowa are all indexed almost as significantly. By utilizing the regional divisions as defined by the *U.S. Statistical Abstract*, the data shows that the Mountain West is the most censorious sub-region, followed by the West North Central and the South Atlantic regions.

The top twenty states in terms of censorship index are widely scattered around the country, yet the Mid-Atlantic, East South Central, and West South Central states are not represented at all among these most censorious states. Both the West North Central and the Mountain West areas have six states among the top twenty. New England and the South Atlantic area are represented by three states each at the top of the list (Table 4.5).

Table 4.4 Number of Incidents and Censorship by Region According to *NIF* Index = percentage of incidents/ percentage population

REGION	INCIDENTS	CENSORSHIP INDEX
NORTHEAST	340	0.77
New England	133	1.16
Mid-Atlantic	207	0.63
MIDWEST	593	1.14
East North Central	360	0.98
West North Central	233	1.51
SOUTH	724	0.97
South Atlantic	466	1.23
East South Central	106	0.80
West South Central	152	0.65
WEST	511	1.11
Mountain West	199	1.67
Pacific	312	0.91

Source: Newsletter on Intellectual Freedom (1981-1990).

Table 4.5 Most Frequent Censorship by State

RANK	NIF		SPLC		ATFL	
	STATE	**INDEX**	**STATE**	**INDEX**	**STATE**	**INDEX**
1	DC	13.08	DC	7.37	WY	9.72
2	WY	9.22	MT	4.15	SD	5.21
3	NE	2.63	ME	3.61	OR	3.85
4	CO	2.48	SD	3.14	VT	3.83
5	WI	2.44	WY	2.44	ND	3.38
6	SD	2.32	CO	1.94	WA	2.68
7	MT	2.31	VA	1.78	AK	2.64
8	VT	2.22	OK	1.76	CO	2.21
9	IA	2.06	MD	1.62	AZ	2.18
10	RI	1.85	IN	1.59	AL	2.16
11	OR	1.81	MA	1.47	NV	1.83
12	ME	1.80	NM	1.44	ME	1.80
13	ND	1.77	NJ	1.43	OK	1.63
14	MN	1.55	NE	1.39	WI	1.48
15	ID	1.50	IL	1.25	KS	1.47
16	FL	1.43	NY	1.23	ID	1.45
17	NH	1.33	WV	1.22	NE	1.40
18	NM	1.28	CA	1.19	MI	1.33
19	AR	1.26	MI	1.19	FL	1.25
20	MD	1.25	ID	1.10	MD	1.22

Note: Censorship News lacks sufficient data to be included in table.
Sources: Newsletter on Intellectual Freedom (1981-1990); *Student Press Law Center Report* (1981-1990); *Attacks on the Freedom to Learn* (1982-1990).

All of this makes for a confusing quilt of regional data. Clearly there has been something happening during the 1980s, but it is difficlt to comb out of the data for how each state reacted to the changes in our national psyche. Furthermore, although it is clear there are differences between states, it is difficult to say how variations in censorship should be compared. Is an index of 1.80 in Maine comparable to a 1.82 in Oregon? Slight variations in the index are probably not significant but large variations may signify where high concentrations of censorship activity exist.

The other reporting sources give insufficient data to compare any regional trends, but *ATFL* does show Midwest and Western states to be the hot spots of censorship incidents (Table 4.5).

CENSORSHIP: WHAT FORMATS ARE TARGETED?

The brunt of censorship, despite technological changes in public media, continues to fall on traditional sources. Similar to Woods' observations in the

1960s and 1970s, books are the most frequent object of attempts at suppression during the 1980s. Books alone make up 41% of all incidents in the *NIF*. When combined with textbooks (required classroom reading) monographic materials make up almost 50% of all objects of censorship reported in the *NIF* (Table 4.6). These attacks on books take place despite continuing complaints about falling literacy rates and fears that children no longer show much interest in reading. Perhaps we are sending the children mixed messages, as if to say, "you should read more books, but not THESE books."

Table 4.6 Number of Challenges According to Format

FORMAT/ SOURCE	NIF	NIF %	CN	ATFL	SPLC
advertisement	27	1.24	2	1	
alternative press					22
art	83	3.82			
art magazine		3			
book	891	40.98	27	217	
comic	32	1.47			
dance	4	0.18			
document	8	0.37			
exhibit	21	0.97	23		
film	174	8.00	2		
game	13	0.60	1		
literary magazine					6
magazine	205	9.43		9	
music	41	1.89			
newspaper	44	2.02			
other	93	4.28	46	25	
play	68	3.13	20		
radio	16	0.74			
speech	70	3.23	3		2
student newspaper	127	5.84	1		169
student publication	24	1.10	2		
television	55	2.53			
textbook	178	8.19	7	11	
yearbook					17

Sources: *Newsletter on Intellectual Freedom* (1981-1990); *Censorship News* (1981-1990); *Attacks on the Freedom to Learn* (1982-1990); *Student Press Law Center Report* (1981-1990).

During this decade, magazines and films have been subjected to extremely high numbers of attacks (Figures 4.2 [a-d]). Frequently during the 1980s these two media have been the objects of organized attacks by local branches of national religious and conservative groups. A typical incident, for example, might

Figure 4.2(a) Proportion of Censorship Challenges According to Format

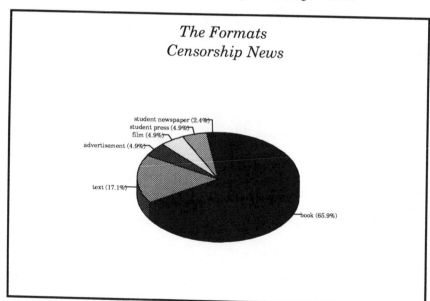

Source: Newsletter on Intellectual Freedom (1981-1990).

Figure 4.2 (b) Proportion of Censorship Challenges According to Format

The Formats
Censorship News

student newspaper (2.4%)
student press (4.9%)
film (4.9%)
advertisement (4.9%)
text (17.1%)
book (65.9%)

Source: Censorship News (1981-1990).

Figure 4.2(c) Proportion of Censorship Challenges According to Format

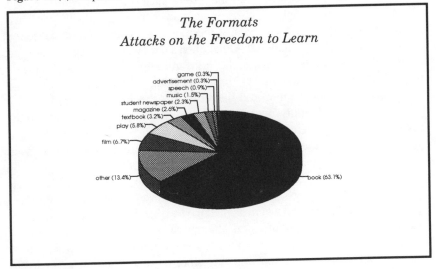

Source: Attacks on the Freedom to Learn (1982-1990).

Figure 4.2(d) Proportion of Censorship Challenges According to Format

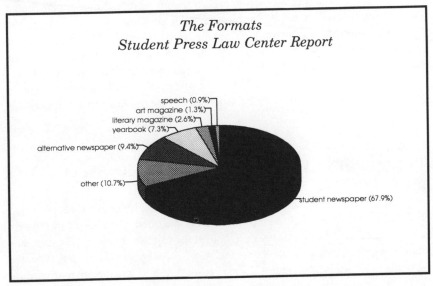

Source: Student Press Law Center Report (1981-1990).

involve a member of the American Family Association lobbying a local convenience store to remove adult magazines such *Playboy*, *Penthouse*, and *High Society* from its shelves. If the request was not complied with, petitions, picketing, and boycotts (or threats of these) are often sufficient to cause the merchants to remove the material. Quite often a frenzy of public concern would seem to develop around one particular store and a few magazine titles, despite the availability of a wide variety of items at other outlets in the area. The justification for this phenomenon has been that the assailed outlet was in a "neighborhood" or "family" location. Retail outlets are not the only institutions subject to magazine censorship. Schools and libraries often experience complaints about publications appealing to teens. *Sports Illustrated*'s swimsuit issue has been a frequent target in the schools during the 1980s.

Films are often the objects of similar actions. Martin Scorcese's *The Last Temptation of Christ*, for example, has been the most frequent target of protest by religious organizations, which wanted the film banned from public viewing. Rarely do protest groups offer an alternative, such as a public forum for discussion of the film and its meaning to the religious faithful. Instead, they simply want to prohibit its showing altogether.

Although print and celluloid are the most censored media, expression of virtually every possible kind has been attacked throughout the decade. Student newspapers are also at high risk, particularly when they have tried to take on issues that were not pleasant for school administrators to deal with. The *Student Press Law Center Report* has the most significant student press data (see Figure 4.2 [d]). The *Newsletter on Intellectual Freedom* reprots a smaller percentage of total censorship accounted for by attacks on the student press, however, the raw data is almost as comparable to that reported by the *SPLC Report* (see Table 4.6 and Figure 4.2 [a]. Works of art also came more and more under attack. This reached a pinnacle after the decade ended (and thus after the purview of this study), when works by Robert Mapplethorpe and Andreas Serrano caused a national reexamination of National Endowment for the Arts (NEA) funding for artistic works.

CENSORSHIP: WHAT INSTITUTIONS ARE AFFECTED?

A look at the institutions most frequently affected by censorship incidents, shows that public education in America is not the open arena for the discussion of ideas that we might hope it would be. Of the top twenty types of institutions reported in *NIF*, nine are educational facilities. Over 60% of all incidents involve schools or libraries (see Table 4.7 and Figures 4.3 [a-d]). Although many would argue that this shows an overwhelming concern for the education of our youth, what it seems to indicate is that we may not be willing to teach the analytical skills necessary to deal with controversial topics. There may be a tendency to

Table 4.7 Number of Censorship Challenges by Institution

INSTITUTION	NIF	CN	ATFL	SPLC
high school	424	10	98	115
university, college	204			106
public library	185	1	7	
high school library	161	1	41	
elementary library	154	7	42	
school	133		4	1
retail outlet	133			1
elementary school	80		30	
junior high library	74	2	49	
school library	73	5	29	
junior high school	70	6	36	3
tv station, program	68			
state committee, state library	49		3	
theater	48			1
museums, centers, exhibits	47			
public forum	46			
newspaper publisher	37	1		
prison	22	1		
radio station, program	21		1	
church	21		1	
book publisher, printer	20			
stage performance	20			
federal government	17			
film company, producer	17			
magazine publisher, printer	16			
none given	15	1	3	
music industry, producer	15		95	
advertising industry	14		11	
school district	13	4	5	
film festival	13		10	
scouts, youth groups	6		12	
labor union	2		23	
library of congress	2			
public schools		2	3	
media center			2	
community college, technical school				8
other				1

Sources: Newsletter on Intellectual Freedom (1981-1985); *Censorship News* (1989-1990); *Attacks on the Freedom to Learn* (1982-1990); *Student Press Law Center Report* (1981-1990).

Figure 4.3(a) Proportion of Censorship Challenges According to Institution

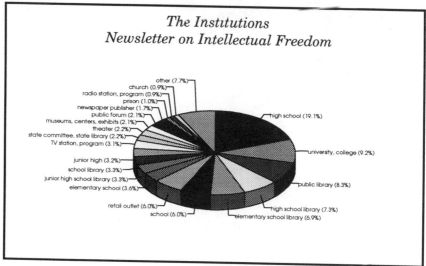

Source: Newsletter on Intellectual Freedom (1981-1990).

Figure 4.3(b) Proportion of Censorship Challenges According to Institution

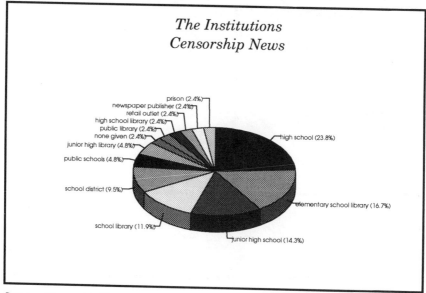

Source: Censorship News (1981-1990).

Figure 4.3(c) Proportion of Censorship Challenges According to Institutution

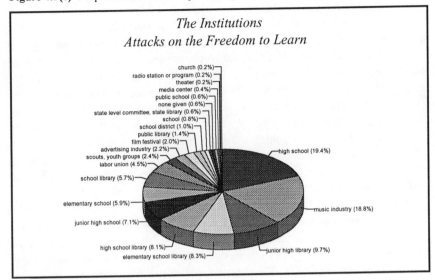

Source: Attacks on the Freedom to Learn (1982-1990).

Figure 4.3(d) Proportion of Censorship Challenges According to Institution

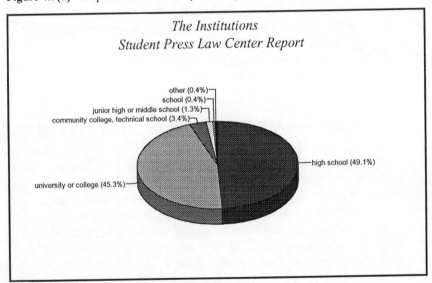

Source: Student Press Law Center Report (1981-1990).

shelter students from difficult subjects, or worse, indoctrinate them to particular points of view.

This preponderance of educational incidents is in step with the fact that books are the most highly censored form of expression. Keeping certain books out of the schools is a very common practice. A phenomenon that other scholars have noted is that modern works that deal realistically with the problems of adolescents and young adults stand a high chance of incurring the wrath of the censor (Fiske 1968). These types of books deal with issues that we wish did not exist and would rather not discuss openly with our children, and thus we attempt to prohibit their expression in children's literature, as if that somehow shields them from these stark realities. For example, currently a similar sentiment is being directed at television programming, which many critics feel is the "cause" of our children's anti-social behavior.

Although most of the educational incidents deal with public grade school education, it is disturbing to see that universities are the location with the second greatest number of occurrences. Discussion of this recent tendency to limit the extent of free expression in higher education has become a popular pastime. Political correctness (PC) is often blamed for this inclination, but this study sees a greater number of so-called conservative issues as the bone of contention, rather than the typical, liberal/PC bias. (see Chapter 4 analysis on objections)

The other reporting sources all show a substantial number of incidents occurring at educational facilities. High schools top the list in all three (*ATFL*, *CN*, and *SPLC Report*) (see Figures 4.3, [b-d]). But as we see in *NIF*, virtually any type of institution is liable to come under censorship attack, including commercial/retail facilities and churches. During this decade, censorship attempts also happened within the publishing industry, including at least one incident which was initiated by one publisher against another.

CENSORSHIP: WHAT ARE THE SOURCES OF ATTEMPTS?

Any type of expression, spoken, written or produced in abstract form, is subject to criticism and formal and informal attempts to suppress or eliminate it can occur at any point in time. Words alone have often caused alarm, as well as ideas. The expression does not have to exist in any tangible form to be attacked. However, most targets of censorship are books and other written or graphic materials (magazines, film, and art). Individuals concerned about intellectual freedom and the preservation of expressive rights know that any one attack on expression is a grave matter, but there is a greater alarm in pervasive challenges against known works, especially those that have passed muster for artistic, literary, or scientific merit. Hence, the focus of many censorship studies has usually been on identifying those specific items that have a significant number of censorship attempts made against them.

A censorship attempt can come from any source. Henry Reichman (1988) has written that censorship is sometimes defined as only that which is an action taken by a governmental authority or other official body. However, research has shown most attempts originate with an individual or group, not a governmental agency. In some circles, it is believed that censorship attempts only originate with more conservative, reactionary individuals and groups. As this study and many others have shown, however, the sources of censorship attempts can emanate from any point on the political spectrum. For instance, Nat Hentoff, a world-renowned author on censorship and free speech, has often excoriated the Council on Interracial Books for Children for practicing censorship, despite its label as a liberal group.

The current study of the four reporting sources on censorship incidents identified sixty-three distinct groups or individuals for which at least one censorship attempt has been discovered in a news report published in *The Newsletter on Intellectual Freedom, Censorship News,* or the *Attacks on the Freedom to Learn* (see Table 4.8). This list was developed by creating an initial set of probable categories, mostly culled from past studies, or that are seemingly obvious such as the parent, principal, or school board categories. As the data was compiled, new items were added to the list when necessary. Any nationally recognized group, such as the Moral Majority or the American Society of Atheists, was given its own category, because the political nature of many censorship battles places power and influence into the hands of groups as well as individuals, and gauging who these groups are was seen as important. Every attempt to group like categories of individuals was made. For example, all ministerial groups were placed in one category, including priests, rabbis, ministers, and lay ministers or church employees. Community professionals, such as doctors, lawyers, dentists, therapists, and pharmacists, occupy positions of social power and influence. Although many have filed a censorship complaint as a private citizen, their special place in the structure of a local community is seen as warranting a separate category.

Of the sixty-three categories on the general list, at least one incident has been reported in *The Newsletter on Intellectual Freedom* for each category, whereas the *Attacks on the Freedom to Learn* has forty-seven categories with at least one recorded incident, and *Censorship News* has only fourteen categories of complainant data (Table 4.8).

The *Student Press Law Center Report* is more narrow in focus. Many of the same groups and individuals from the initial list of complainants are also included in the *SPLC* portion of this list, such as parent, minister, and principal. There are twenty-three categories that are included on both lists, and five that are only on the *SPLC* list (see Table 4.8). Because the *SPLC Report* records censorship of the student press exclusively, three separate categories for "alumnus," "student editors or staff," and "student government" were seen as necessary. The data also recorded incidents where censorship attempts were

Table 4.8 Complainants Listed in Censorship Attempts

COMPLAINANT/SOURCE	NIF	CN	ATFL	SPLC
parent	611	9	123	3
citizen	224	2	28	6
minister	220	4	7	1
principal	209	1	6	72
various organized groups	149	4	70	
school board	135	8	1	6
government official	103		4	
student	103		2	14
university official	101		3	54
superintendent	74	1		
law enforcement official	69			
teacher, professor	65	3	1	13
city council, county commissioner	62			
businesses	51		1	
librarian	38	3	40	
TV station officials	34			
Eagle Forum	33	4		
newspaper, editor, staff	32		3	
state government official	27		2	3
art museum, music hall, exhibit officials	25	2		
school personnel	25	1	9	
radio station officials	23			
Moral Majority	22		1	3
Citizens for Excellence in Education	20		7	
American Family Association	19		2	
publisher, printer, distributor	19			1
prison official	18	1		
ethnic groups	17		1	
library board	17		3	
Christian Broadcasting Network	16			
NAACP	15			8
none given	15	2	11	2
state board, state library	15			
U.S. Senator/ Congressman	15		16	
parents groups (PTA, PTO)	14		12	
Anti-Defamation League	13			3
Citizens for Decency Through Law	12		1	
mayor, city manager	12			
National Organization For Women	12	3		
Catholic League for Religious and Civil Rights	11		2	
professional	11		14	
Concerned Women for America	10		6	
feminists	10		1	1
library staffer	10		1	
anti-abortion groups	8		38	
arts council	8		1	
Profamily Forum	8			

Table 4.8 (continued)

COMPLAINANT/SOURCE	NIF	CN	ATFL	SPLC
labor union	6			
Morality in Media	6		1	
American Society of Atheists	5			
celebrity	5			
National Coalition Against Pornography	5		9	
Educational Research Analysts	4		7	
gay activists	4		1	
Women Against Pornography	4		1	
Accuracy in Media/ Academia	3		6	
Church of Scientology	3		7	
Motion Picture Association of America	3		1	
National Coalition on Television Violence	3			
advertiser	2		7	2
Focus on the Family	2		2	
youth groups or scouts officials	2		1	
Klu Klux Klan				
faculty advisor				7
named individual				2
Parent's Music Resource Center				1
school alumnus				1
school official		4	17	26
student government				16
student paper, editor, staff				6

Sources: Newsletter on Intellectual Freedom (1981-1990); *Censorship News* (1981-1990); *Attacks on the Freedom to Learn* (1982-1990); *Student Press Law Center Report* (1981-1990).

made by the Parent's Music Resource Center and by a person named in the article in question that have not been recorded in any report of the other three publications.

Censorship by Individuals

Censorship reports often include more than one person or group who has objected to an expressive work. Although there are 2174 separate incidents reported in *The Newsletter on Intellectual Freedom* for this period, there are 2,818 complainants, which yields an average of 1.3 complainants per incident. Likewise, there are 344 separate incidents reported in the *Attacks on the Freedom to Learn* for this same time period and 485 complainants, which yields an average of 1.41 complainants for each incident in this publication. *Censorship News* also has more recorded complainants than incidents (forty-one incidents and forty-seven complainants for an average of slightly more than 1 per incident).

Although the magnitude of complainants in each category varies across the four sources, there are some striking similarities as well as differences. All three sources of book censorship record "Parent" as the number one complainant, whereas the *SPLC Report* covering the student press found the "Principal" as the number one category, ranking "Parent" as a distant thirteenth (see Figures 4.4 [a-d]). Four categories, "Parent," "Citizen," "locally organized groups," and "school officials" (a category for complainants where the actual title of the school official has not been identified in the report), occur in the top ten of all three book censorship sources where only "school official" was also ranked as high in the *SPLC Report*. When an examination of the twenty most frequent complaints from each source is made, the number of simultaneous complainants increases slightly, with "Principal" the only additional category ranked as high on all four lists. This appears to indicate some uniqueness of each source.

This study shows that parents are the number one complainant. *The Newsletter on Intellectual Freedom* records 611 incidents of parental complaints, which occurred in 22.4% of all the incidents reported (see Figure 4.4 [a]). Likewise, the *Attacks on the Freedom to Learn* has found 35.75% of all reported incidents to have originated with a parent (Figure 4.4 [c]) and *Censorship News* records 22% of all incidents involved a parental complaint (Figure 4.4 [b]). By contrast, only 1.3% of all censorship attempts listed in *Student Press Law Center Report* are as the result of a parent's complaint (Figure 4.4 [d]). Table 4.8 also shows that ministers and citizens play a significant role in filing censorship challenges. The *NIF* records 8.1% of all complaints originate with a minister and 8.2% are made by a local citizen. *Censorship News* also attributes 8.5% of all attempts to a minister, but only 4.3% to a local citizen. However, the *Attacks on the Freedom to Learn* points to other sources. Their data indicates that locally organized groups and librarians play a much more significant role in censorship than ministers and individual citizens (14.4% and 8.2%, respectively).

Comparative data of the attributes was also possible. A spreadsheet has been used to compile all the statistics of each attribute and it allows cross tabulations. For instance, not only can the number of complainants be measured but Table 4.9 also shows that the types of objections for each complainant were possible to tabulate. Only the three most frequent complainants are included here, but it indicates that parents objected to sexual content and profanity the most, as reported by the *NIF*, whereas citizens and ministers have seen sexual content and obscenity as the two most difficult subjects. This data closely parallels the reported totals of all incidents. The "occult" and "anti-Christian" objections rank high with all three categories of complainants in addition to several sexually related objections.

Figure 4.4(a) Proportion of Censorship Challenges According to Complainant

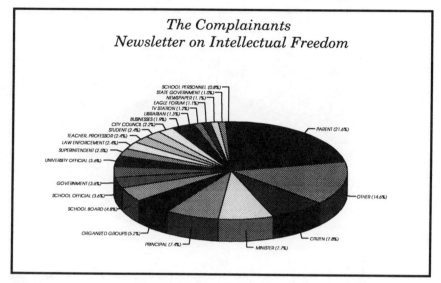

Source: Newsletter on Intellectual Freedom (1981-1990).

Figure 4.4(b) Proportion of Censorship Challenges According to Complainant

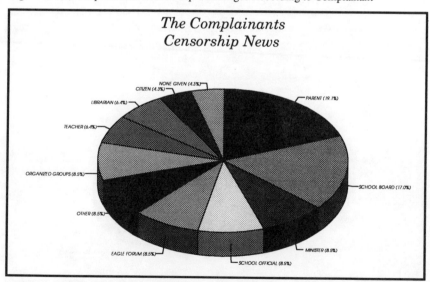

Source: Censorship News (1981-1990).

Figure 4.4(c) Proportion of Censorship Challenges According to Complainant

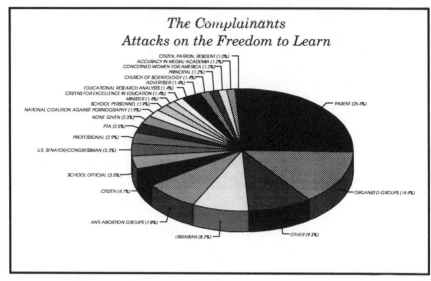

Source: Attacks on the Freedom to Learn (1982-1990).

Figure 4.4(d) Proportion of Censorship Challenges According to Complainant

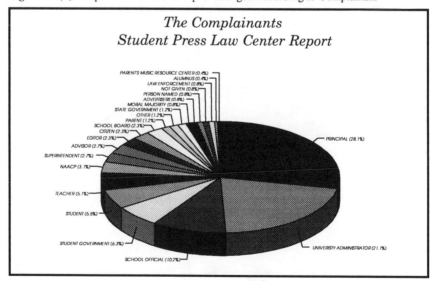

Source: Student Press Law Center Report (1981-1990).

Table 4.9 Most Frequent Objections of the Top Three Complainant Categories

NEWSLETTER ON INTELLECTUAL FREEDOM

	PARENT		MINISTER		CITIZEN	
1	sexual content	213	sexual content	60	sexual content	56
2	profanity	156	obscene	38	obscene	39
3	occult	62	occult	35	profanity	22
4	anti-Christian	51	profanity	32	homosexuality	20
5	obscene	49	anti-Christian	32	occult	19
6	inappropriate	37	homosexuality	17	inappropriate	15
7	too violent	33	no reason given	12	anti-Christian	13
8	no reason given	31	immoral	10	nudity	12
9	secular humanist	24	abortion	9	abortion	11
10	homosexuality	23	nudity	8	drugs	9

CENSORSHIP NEWS

	PARENT		SCHOOL BOARD		MINISTER	
1	sexual content	3	no reason given	5	profanity	3
2	anti-family	3	inappropriate	1	feminist	2
3	anti-Christian	3	anti-American	1	obscene	2
4	profanity	3	anti-Semitic	1	anti-family	1
5	anti-nuclear	1	anti-Christian	1	anti-Christian	1
6	too contro-versial	1	obscene	1		
7	disrespectful to authority	1	profanity	1		
8	abortion	1				
9	immoral	1				
10	fosters disrespect	1				

ATTACKS ON THE FREEDOM TO LEARN

	PARENT		LOCALLY ORGANIZED GROUPS		LIBRARIAN	
1	profanity	15	racist	2	causes disorder	2
2	sexual content	11	causes disorder	2	racist	2
3	occult	11	sexual content	1	negative	1
4	anti-Christian	9	homosexuality	1	Marxist, communist	1
5	Secular Humanist	6	Marxist, communist	1	anti-Christian	1
6	too violent	6	violates separation of church and state	1	disrespectful to authorities	1
7	inappropriate	5	anti-Christian	1	anti-family	1
8	racist	5	disrespectful to authority	1	political tone	1
9	obscene	4	anti-family	1	lack of value	1
10	negative	4	not approved	1	feminist	1

Table 4.9 (continued)

STUDENT PRESS LAW CENTER REPORT					
PRINCIPAL		UNIVERSITY ADMINISTRATOR		SCHOOL OFFICIAL	
1 too critical of school	21	too critical of school	14	racist	3
2 sexually explicit	11	too negative image of school	8	violates separation of church and state	3
3 inappropriate	10	abortion	4	contraceptives	3
4 too negative image of school		pornographic	4	author, article violates law	2
5 causes disorder	5	libelous	4	abortion	2
6 inaccurate	5	sexually explicit	4	drugs	2
7 racist	3	contra-ceptives	3	not approved	2
8 ridicules individuals or groups	3	anti-Christian	3	profanity	2
9 not approved	3	sexist	2	inappropriate	2
10 libelous	2	inaccurate	2	nudity	2

Sources: Newsletter on Intellectual Freedom (1981-1990); *Censorship News* (1981-1990); *Attacks on the Freedom to Learn* (1982-1990); *Student Press Law Center Report* (1981-1990).

Censorship by Organized Groups

During the data-gathering stage, the reports indicated that many communities experienced organized efforts at the grass roots level for the express purpose of influencing the outcome of that one controversy. These groups often have emotionally laden titles such as "Save Our Schools" or "Concerned Citizens for Quality Education." These names usually are not readily identified with a known national organization such as the Moral Majority, Citizens for Excellence in Education, or the American Family Association who often help mobilize such grass roots organizations. If the news report indicated any national affiliation, the category for the national group was incremented. If no such linkage was shown, a category of "locally organized group" was used rather than the actual name of that organization. Table 4.10 shows that locally organized groups accounted for 5.3% of all the complaints reported in the *NIF*.

The Newsletter on Intellectual Freedom contains a more significant body of data on the level of activity by powerful national interests. As compared with the other three sources, it reports censorship incidents originating with twenty-three nationally recognized organizations (see Table 4.10). *Censorship News* lists only one (The Eagle Forum), *Attacks on the Freedom to Learn* sixteen groups (Table 4.10), and the *SPLC Report* three (NAACP, Moral Majority, and Parent's Music Resource Center). These organizations account for 229 incidents altogether or 8.1% of the *NIF* total. The Eagle Forum is the most significant, ranking seventeenth of sixty-three categories of complainants and recording thirty-three censorship attempts or 1.21% of the total. The Moral Majority, Citizens for Excellence in Education, and the American Family Association almost attain a similar stature, ranking twenty-one, twenty-five, and twenty-six respectively. These four organizations are responsible for ninety-four of all the censorship challenges in The *NIF* (or 3.5% of all recorded attempts). As Table 4.10 indicates, sixteen of these twenty-three nationally organized groups are considered to be conservative in their philosophy or outlook, whereas only four are considered to be liberal. Four groups, the Church of Scientology, the National Coalition Against TV Violence, Motion Picture Association of America, and the Parent's Music Resource Center are difficult to classify.

Table 4.10 Number of Censorship Attempts Made by Organized Groups According to Political Orientation (PO; c = conservative, l = liberal, u = unknown)

GROUP/ SOURCE	PO	NIF	SPLC	CN	ATFL
Eagle Forum	c	33		4	
Moral Majority	c	22	3		1
Citizens for Excellence in Education	c	20			7
American Family Association	c	20			2
Christian Broadcasting Network	c	15			
Citizens for Decency Through Law	c	12			1
Catholic League for Religious and Civil Rights	c	11			2
Concerned Women for America	c	10			6
Profamily Forum	c	8			
Morality in Media	c	6			1
National Coalition Against Pornography	c	5			9
Women Against Pornography	c	4			1
Educational Research Analysts	c	4			7
Accuracy in Media/Academia	c	3			6
Focus on the Family	c	2			2
Klu Klux Klan	c	1			
N.A.A.C.P.	l	14			8
Anti-Defamation League	l	13			3
National Organization for Women	l	12			3
American Society of Atheists	l	5			
National Coalition on Television Violence	u	3			1
Motion Picture Association of America	u	3			
Church of Scientology	u	3			7
Parents Music Resource Center	u		1		
locally organized groups	u	149		4	70

Sources: Newsletter on Intellectual Freedom (1981-1990); Student Press Law Center Report (1981-1990); Censorship News; (1981-1990); Attacks on the Freedom to Learn (1982-1990).

CENSORSHIP: WHAT ARE THE OBJECTIONS?

The types of objections made against books and other expressive works are also quite varied and diverse. Fifty-seven reasons why a work may be considered inappropriate by at least one person and reported in one of the four sources studied have been identified over the course of the project (see Table 4.11). Every attempt to group like reasons into categories has been made. For instance, complaints about a work that in some way attacked or ridiculed religion, including "anti-Christian," "sacrilegious," or "anti-religious" have been grouped in one category. However, complaints about offensive commentary against Jews or Judaism have been included in the "anti-Semitic" category.

Table 4.11   Reasons Given in Censorship Attempts

REASON/ SOURCE	NIF	CN	ATFL	SPLC
sexual content-based	533	6	41	22
profane	361	15	49	8
obscene	257	3	8	10
anti-religious, anti-Christian, sacrilegious	136	6	20	6
occult, witchcraft, devil worship	133		36	2
nudity, revealing clothing	121		5	8
inappropriate	116	4	11	13
homosexuality	82	1	6	10
violence	72		11	
none given	64	7	7	
racist	64		14	21
abortion	59	1	2	8
too critical of school	55			63
ridicules individuals or groups; ethnic slurs	54		14	8
too critical of government	52			
violation of law or regulation	52			5
drugs	49		1	5
immoral; lack of value	49	6	5	4
political tone	46		15	
Secular Humanist, New Age	43		9	
inaccurate, misleading, poor grammar	43	1	1	17
anti-family, anti-family values	42	3	38	
causes disorder, fights, security problems	40		14	10
sexist	39		1	8
controversial	35	3	6	
disrespectful to police or authority; fosters disrespect	35	4	75	1
violence against women	34		4	3
too negative	33		7	

Table 4.11 (continued)

REASON/SOURCE	NIF	CN	ATFL	SPLC
promotes a religion, violates separation of church and state	31		10	5
too liberal	29	4	2	3
anti-American	27	1	3	1
anti-Semitic	26	1	2	
Marxist, communist, socialist	25		3	
contraceptives	22	1	3	11
suicide	20		4	1
feminist	20		3	5
not approved; violates time, space regulations	19		3	5
libelous	17			26
promotes evolution; does not promote creation	15		1	
offensive to named individual	14		2	
anti-business; anti-wealthy	14			1
alcohol	13	7	3	
violates privacy, individual rights	9		1	3
anti-nuclear power, anti-war, anti-military	7	1	1	
copyright, trademark infringement	7			2
A.I.D.S.	6		3	3
prostitution	3		1	
violates fair trial	3		2	
flag desecration	3		1	
too conservative	1		1	2
violation of free speech	1		3	
too critical of labor union	1			
too critical of student government				6
other				5
violation of school policy				4
unsigned editorial				4
disagreement with subject matter				2

Sources: Newsletter on Intellectual Freedom (1981-1990); *Censorship News* (1981-1990); *Attacks on the Freedom to Learn* (1982-1990); *Student Press Law Center Report* (1981-1990).

Other multi-reason categories include:

--Violence and horror or too frightening; too bloody or gory
--Inaccurate or misleading; poor grammar (often charges made against student journalism)
--Racist; offensive to blacks; promotes antiquated ideas about blacks; promotes display of the Confederate flag (similar issues related to insensitivities towards Black Americans)
--Anti-business; anti-wealthy, upper class; pro-labor union (similar charges concerning division of the classes and anti-wealth)
--Promotes evolution; does not promote creation science (two similar arguments)
--Secular humanism; New Age; values clarification (charges often made together about the same texts)

It is conceivable that one category could have been created for several of the sexually related categories included in this study. However, a separate classification was made for each of the following objections because they are seen as uniquely different and important to study individually:

--Pornographic or obscene
--Profanity, vulgar language
--Sexually explicit or sexual content
--Nudity or revealing clothing
--Homosexuality
--Prostitution
--Immoral
--Contraceptives

Each of these is seen as a distinct and separate complaint. Many individuals do not view obscenity as different from sexual explicitness or content. The language used has often seemed interchangeable. However, if a reason was given that mentioned something objectionable about sexual content but did not explicitly call the work obscene or pornography, only the "sexually explicit, sexual content" category was incremented. If the complainant labeled the item "obscene" or "pornographic" no attempt to apply a legal definition was made, but simply recorded as an "obscene" complaint reason. Rather than making an attempt to guess what each complaint meant, the data recorded took the reason reported at face value. The categories "homosexuality," "prostitution," and "contraceptives" are specific types of sexually oriented content and, furthermore, complainants will most often argue that the offending item promotes these types of activities. "Nudity" as a category applies most often to art work or a graphic representation in the work rather than written or spoken content. Several incidents recorded complaints that the book or other work was "immoral" and an analysis of the report indicates sexual content as the basis for the charge. Three other categories have a sexual connotation or aspect but are seen as important issues in their own right or too remotely removed from a sexually content-based complaint to be lumped in with data for the analysis of this type of attack: "abortion," "AIDS," and "violence against women." These have been recorded and analyzed separately.

Based on the data of this study, sexually related complaints appear to be the most troublesome for intellectual freedom concerns. A sexually related complaint, for instance, is the most frequent complaint recorded in the *Newsletter on Intellectual Freedom* (sexual content) and in *Censorship News* (profanity), the second most frequent in the *Attacks on the Freedom to Learn* (profanity), and third in the *Student Press Law Center Report* (sexual content) (Figures 4.5 [a-d]).

The *Newsletter on Intellectual Freedom*, with the most significant data, shows that, for the 1980s, the eight sexually related categories account for 1,428

Figure 4.5(a) Proportion of Censorship Challenges According to Reason

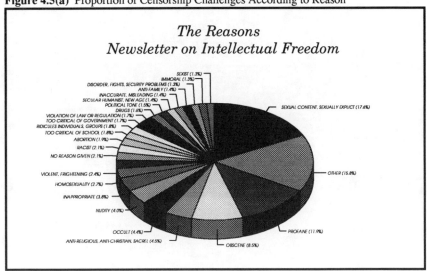

Source: Newsletter on Intellectual Freedom (1981-1990).

Figure 4.5(b) Proportion of Censorship Challenges According to Reason

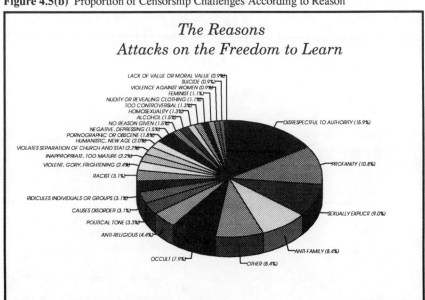

Source: Attacks on the Freedom to Learn (1982-1990).

Figure 4.5(c) Proportion of Censorship Challenges According to Reason

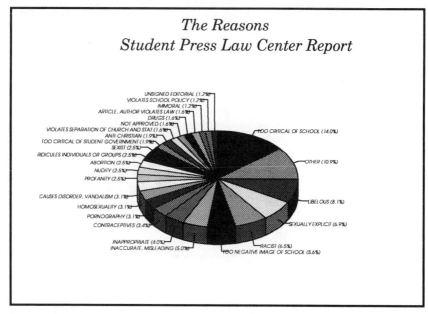

The Reasons
Censorship News

LACK OF VALUE OR MORAL VALUE (0.9%)
SUICIDE (0.9%)
VIOLENCE AGAINST WOMEN (0.9%)
FEMINIST (1.1%)
NUDITY OR REVEALING CLOTHING (1.1%)
TOO CONTROVERSIAL (1.3%)
HOMOSEXUALITY (1.3%)
ALCOHOL (1.5%)
NO REASON GIVEN (1.5%)
NEGATIVE, DEPRESSING (1.5%)
PORNOGRAPHIC OR OBSCENE (1.8%)
HUMANISTIC, NEW AGE (2.0%)
VIOLATES SEPARATION OF CHURCH AND STAT (2.2%)
INAPPROPRIATE, TOO MATURE (2.2%)
VIOLENT, GORY, FRIGHTENING (2.4%)
RACIST (3.1%)
RIDICULES INDIVIDUALS OR GROUPS (3.1%)
CAUSES DISORDER (3.1%)
POLITICAL TONE (3.3%)
ANTI-RELIGIOUS (4.4%)
OCCULT (7.9%)
OTHER (8.4%)
ANTI-FAMILY (8.4%)
SEXUALLY EXPLICIT (9.0%)
PROFANITY (10.8%)
DISRESPECTFUL TO AUTHORITY (15.9%)

Source: Censorship News (1981-1990).

Figure 4.5(d) Proportion of Censorship Challenges According to Reason

The Reasons
Student Press Law Center Report

UNSIGNED EDITORIAL (1.2%)
VIOLATES SCHOOL POLICY (1.2%)
IMMORAL (1.2%)
ARTICLE, AUTHOR VIOLATES LAW (1.6%)
DRUGS (1.6%)
NOT APPROVED (1.6%)
VIOLATES SEPARATION OF CHURCH AND STAT (1.6%)
ANTI-CHRISTIAN (1.9%)
TOO CRITICAL OF STUDENT GOVERNMENT (1.9%)
SEXIST (2.5%)
RIDICULES INDIVIDUALS OR GROUPS (2.5%)
ABORTION (2.5%)
NUDITY (2.5%)
PROFANITY (2.5%)
CAUSES DISORDER, VANDALISM (3.1%)
HOMOSEXUALITY (3.1%)
PORNOGRAPHY (3.1%)
CONTRACEPTIVES (3.4%)
INAPPROPRIATE (4.0%)
INACCURATE, MISLEADING (5.0%)
TOO NEGATIVE IMAGE OF SCHOOL (5.6%)
RACIST (6.5%)
SEXUALLY EXPLICIT (6.9%)
LIBELOUS (8.1%)
OTHER (10.9%)
TOO CRITICAL OF SCHOOL (14.0%)

Source: Student Press Law Center Report (1981-1990).

attempts, or 50.7% of all the complaints recorded in the *NIF* incidents. The statistics for the other publications are also substantial: *Censorship News*-- twenty-six sexual content-based complaints out of seventy-one (36.6% of the total); *Attacks on the Freedom to Learn*--114 of 454 complaints (25.1% of the total); and the *Student Press Law Center Report*--seventy-three of 321 complaints (22.1% of the total) (Table 4.11).

This shows that sexual content and issues preoccupy the censor according to the data of this study. Figures 4.5 [a-d] show a comparison of the most frequent reasons why an expressive work has been found objectionable. The five most frequent sexual content-based categories in the *NIF* account for almost half (48.1%) of all objections. These same reasons recorded in *CN* total twenty-six of the seventy-one complaints, which is the sum total of all complaints in this publication. Sexually related categories are less prominent, although still significant, in the *Attacks on the Freedom to Learn* data. Four of these categories are among the most frequent and they account for 28.8% of that total. The *Student Press Law Center Report* has shown that sexual content as well as control of the student press is a problem. The eight sexual content categories total more than the "too critical of school objection," the most frequent complaint used to control student publications. Sexual explicitness or sexual content is high on each list: first in *NIF* data and accounting for 18.5% of all complaints alone and third in the other three source lists (Figures 4.5 [a-d]). Profanity or vulgar language is also a major concern: first in the *Censorship News* list, comprising 21.1% of all *CN* complaints; second in both the *NIF* and *ATFL* lists (361 of 2,818 *NIF* complaints or 12.8% of the total and 49 of 455 *ATFL* complaints, or 10.8% of that total).

Although it had been thought that political issues and the occult would be very dominant in the statistics prior to the data collection, the occult and its related complaints (witchcraft, devil worship, etc.) account for only 133 of the reasons given in the *Newsletter on Intellectual Freedom* (4.3% of the total) and thirty-six of the reasons in the *Attacks on the Freedom to Learn* (7.93% of the total). *Censorship News* has not recorded an incident with an occult theme and the *Student Press Law Center Report* lists only two such incidents out of 321 complaints made (0.62% of the *SPLC* total). When the totals for the political categories in the table are combined, in each of the four sources, the sum total of political content-based objections does not account for more than 5% of all complaints.

Many non-sexually related issues do constitute a major concern by individuals and groups, however. The remaining categories can be viewed as part of the schism in society between left and right political spectrums, at least in part. Conservatives and fundamentalist Christians have often been concerned about the erosion of the family values taught by a strict interpretation of the Bible. Of the total possible reasons, the following objections fit within what is seen as a call to return to traditional values:

--Secular humanism
--Promotes abortion
--Anti-Christian
--Disrespectful to authority
--Anti-family
--Anti-American
--Occult, witchcraft, devil worship
--Promotes evolution, does not promote creation scince
--Flag desecration
--Anti-war, anti-military, anti-nuclear power

On the other side of the political fence, liberals often complain about the unfair treatment of minorities and suppressed groups. Their concern is for a more pluralistic society. Liberals are also concerned about erosions in human rights and civil liberties. Of the total possible objections, the following fit within what is seen as a call for pluralism or liberal views:

--Encourages or promotes violence against women
--Encourages or promotes a religion or violates the principle of separation of church and state
--Ridicules individuals or groups (a Category used to record complaints about ethnic slurs other than against Blacks and Jews)
--Sexist, exploits women
--Violation of free speech
--Racist
--Interferes with a fair trial
--Anti-semitic
--Too critical of labor unions
--Violation of individual's privacy

If all incidents in the *NIF* are considered, the traditional values categories, other than sexual content-based ones, account for 534 complaints or 18.9% of the total reported. Concerns about content that is occult related or anti-Christian made up 269 of that total or 50.4% of all traditional values categorical objections. Abortion, secular humanism, and anti-family content also are relatively significant issues that arise in the data. Comparable data in the other resources are similar to this result: *Censorship News*--eighteen of 71; *Attacks on the Freedom to Learn*--188 of 454; *SPLC Report*--twenty of 321 (Table 4.11).

Compared with the identified traditional values, pluralistic or liberal categories appear to be less of a concern as measured by the reported cases. Of all recorded incidents in the *NIF,* these categories totaled 262 of 2,818, or 9.3% of all complaints, about half as many as the traditional values categories. Racism (sixty-four complaints) and ethnic slurs or attacks on the status of individuals or groups (fifty-four) are the primary issues found in this group of categories. Sexism (thirty-nine), violence against women (thirty-four), and promoting a religion (thirty-one) are also troublesome topics (Table 4.5). Comparable data in the other resources studied is somewhat similar: *Censorship News*--one of seventy-one complaints; *Attacks on the Freedom to Learn*--forty-nine of 454; *SPLC Report*--fifty of 321.

As mentioned earlier, the supposition about censorship has usually been that it is committed by conservatives. In a recent article in *The National Review* intended to show this is not true, Stephen Bates (1993) introduces his argument by echoing this belief, "It has become one of journalism's autumn perennials: Book-burners are conspiring to regulate our children to ignorance. Read a bit further in the articles and, almost invariably, the would-be censors turn out to be conservatives." Although Bates purports to show that at least textbook censorship is committed by liberals more than conservatives, our findings indicate that the overwhelming tone of all types of censorship is decidedly conservative. If just the complaints that are sexually related are combined with those that project traditional values, they account for 1,962 of the 2,818 complaints alone. Not factored into this is any other category that may fit within a conservative tradition, such as "promotes drug abuse," "promotes alcohol abuse," or any conservative political category. These conservative complaints account for 69.6% of the total. These are objections that focus on a diverse set of subjects, mostly controversial, but that are the substance of personal life experiences of many people in society and which become ready theme materials for fiction, nonfiction, and other expressive works.

In contrast, the liberal or pluralistic categories listed focus on two issues: objections to content that subjugate or ridicule groups or individuals, especially minorities or groups traditionally treated in a secondary role in society: racism-Blacks; anti-Semitism--Jews; sexism and violence against women--women; ethnic slurs--ethnic groups; or objections to violations of what is seen as First Amendment rights. These liberal objections account for 269 of the 2818 or only 9.3% of all recorded objections (see Table 4.11).

This analysis of the conservative or liberal orientation of the data is problematic, however. Individuals identify themselves as conservative or liberal because of beliefs held dearly. Specific complaints about a book or other work are manifestations of those beliefs. However, the analysis of who the censors are, as identified in this study, does not show whether conservatives practice censorship more than liberals. Many of the most frequent categories, such as parent, principal, student, and the like do not lend themselves readily to a conservative or liberal label. It is very conceivable that a liberal parent could object to their child having access to a book with sexual explicitness and make a formal complaint. The conclusions that information on complaints can lead to cannot show if conservatives as a class of people are more censorious than liberals. Some data suggested this, however. As mentioned earlier, a comparison of conservative and liberal groups that can be readily labeled shows that four times as many conservative groups as liberal groups are found to be involved in a censorship controversy. However, only 239 cases, at the most, can be attributed to these groups (see Table 4.10).

Instead of a focus on individual or group categories, it is more illustrative if the orientation of the data is determined from an analysis of the tone of the complaints made. It has been shown that at least eleven of the categories of complaints can be readily identified as conservative or traditional values concerns. At least two of the political objections ("Marxism" and "too liberal") can be attributed to conservative opinion. This compares to the eight categories that can be labeled liberal. The remaining categories are, therefore, in question. Eight are sexually related. Are concerns about sexual content liberal or conservative? Whereas a liberal individual could find a work objectionable based on sexual content, it is generally accepted that such objections are conservative in nature. The data of this study shows that sexual content-based categories and those of traditional values account for 69.6% of the total complaints made, whereas the liberal categories account for 9.3%. This indicates clearly a conservative tone to the censorship attempts made.

CENSORSHIP: WHAT ARE THE RESULTS?

The outcomes of the censorship attempts recorded by this research are varied and numerous as well. An initial set of result possibilities has been developed in much the same manner as the other attributes (see Table 4.12). As the data were compiled, unique result categories or final outcomes that did not fit within the initial set of results were added to the list. Every attempt to group like results was made.

The nature of the data gathering made the recording of the results somewhat problematic. The reports of censorship challenges occurred at any point in the life of the attempt. For example, 289 complaints in the *NIF* (or 13.29% of the total recorded) were reported at the initial stage of the complaint (Table 4.12), that is, that a complaint was filed, but that no action had yet been taken or the item was still under review. Over the ten years of coverage studied, follow-up data was tracked in order to record the last or final outcome reported. Although many more reports in the four periodicals originally listed the result as a complaint filed with no action taken, if the incident was located in a later issue of the corresponding censorship source, the more up to date result was substituted and the initial result recorded was removed from the collection and analysis.

This presents another problem and one of comprehensive coverage. Because the research examined only ten years of censorship reports, from January 1981 through December 1990, not all final results could be included. Some incidents reported in late 1990 may have had a final disposition reported in 1991 or later. Furthermore, many incidents do not have a follow-up report. Often the stated initial result was one that appeared to be less than final, but, if no other outcome

Table 4.12   Results of Censorship Attempts

RESULT/ SOURCE	NIF	SPLC	CN	ATFL
REVIEW COMMITTEE				
kept	100			
restricted use	21		1	
required parental permission	13			11
moved item to higher level	5			
banned, canceled	30			2
SCHOOL/ LIBRARY BOARD				
kept	288	24		2
restricted use	26		5	13
required parental permission	24			1
banned, canceled	87			9
READING LISTS				
kept on required	8			
kept on optional	6		2	
moved from required to optional	13		6	
kept with alternative available	12		4	
OTHER RESULTS: SUCCESSFUL ATTEMPTS				
banned	393	42	21	78
canceled	115	2		18
cut, pasted, glued over	69	11	3	4
rejected for inclusion	50	5	5	2
ban upheld in court	37	14		
editor, staff suspended or fired	33	37	1	2
people involved threatened with arrest or arrested	33			
destroyed/ vandalized	30	3	1	
student suspended or expelled	28	17		
editor, staff, advisor resigned	14	3		1
item stolen, checked out and not returned, etc.	12	8		1
police, authority seized or canceled	10			
librarian, author, etc. threatened or harmed	6	1		
copies seized		20		
blank page or "censored" printed		2		
newspaper closed permanently		1		
OTHER ACTION: UNSUCCESSFUL				
item kept	75		8	4

Table 4.12 (continued)

RESULT/SOURCE	NIF	SPLC	CN	ATFL
OTHER ACTION: UNSUCCESSFUL				
court struck down ban	62	28	3	
complaint withdrawn	2	1		
library added item to collection	1			
OTHER ACTION: PARTIALLY SUCCESSFUL				
item moved to higher level	31		1	16
new guidelines for selection, removal	30	20	1	
item delayed from release	25	9		
funding reduced or eliminated	18	12		2
legislature introduced or passed legislation against such items	10			
substituted or abridged	8		1	14
program changed time, location, station	3			
newspaper closed temporarily		5		
restricted to campus distribution		4		
OTHER ACTION: STILL PENDING, OTHER				
no action taken or mentioned	15		1	
complaint filed, no action taken	289	33	8	
boycotted, protested	84	7		
citizen, student, author defended item		36		
decision postponed	12			
testimony against item	10			
parties settled out of court		7		

Sources: Newsletter on Intellectual Freedom (1981-1990); *Student Press Law Center Report* (1981-1990); *Censorship News* (1981-1990); *Attacks on the Freedom to Learn* (1982-1990).

could be discovered in subsequent reports, the last, most progressive disposition in the chain of possible outcomes was recorded. For example, if the report indicated that a review committee recommended a course of action, such as, that an item be restricted to older students or adults, it would appear that a governing board or other authority would have to vote to accept or reject the recommendation. If no follow-up report indicated any further action, the corresponding result for the review committee was incremented in the data file.

In establishing this list, an attempt to simplify it could have been made. For instance, several of the result categories clearly state that the item was banned ("Review Committee recommended item be banned," "School Board voted to ban the item," "Item banned or removed," "Item canceled," "Courts upheld ban or removal," etc.) (see Table 4.12). The same is true for materials kept or not banned, or for items kept, removed, or changed on a reading list. However, it is believed that doing so would not give a clear enough picture of what happened.

A distinction was been made among the authoritative bodies. A review committee generally does not have the same authority as a school board or library board, yet their recommendation is often the most crucial step. It is believed that more useful statistics can come from separate data for review committees from that of school boards or library boards. Several categories are the same for review committees as they are for school boards or library boards. This study was designed to examine the impact and differences of both of these types of authoritative bodies.

A distinction was been noted between individual authority and group authority. It was found that not every institution places such challenges through a formal review process nor up for a vote of approval by a governing board. The study included data from all types of institutions, such as retail outlets, publishers, radio and television stations, and theaters, many of which do not have any form of governing authority or review process. Even those organizations that do, such as schools and libraries, often experience review or disposition by an individual rather than a board, for instance by the librarian, principal, superintendent, or teacher. As the data was gathered, decision categories for dispositions made by an individual rather than boards have been recorded separately. The category "Item banned or removed" has been used to include the results of cases wherein individual authorities, not boards, have acted to ban a book or other item. This data represents decisions made by businessmen, principals, librarians, teachers, and so forth, acting in their official capacity, but without mention of a governing board's decision or for reports that did not indicate who made the decision.

The results found here are also classified into four categories of success (see Table 4.13). The first group are those results that successfully concluded the censorship challenge and caused the book or material to be banned, the content to be altered in some way, or complete access to be denied. From an intellectual freedom point of view, this can be considered a negative outcome because the censorship attempt has been successful. Included here are not only results such as an item being banned or canceled but also materials being edited, cut out, or covered over to remove the offending content, and such results as the item being stolen or checked out but not returned. Such outcomes are an effective form of censorship, although they may not meet every aspect of a formal definition. Also included in this category are results that involve a detrimental outcome for an individual, such as a student, teacher, librarian, student editor, publication adviser, and others who either defended the item, created it, or were responsible for its care and access. These are instances where individuals have been fired from their jobs or positions of authority, or suspended or expelled from school, or forced to resign as a result of the censorship attempt, and in each case, the item in question was also banned, removed, or canceled. The action taken against the

Table 4.13   Results of Censorship Challenges Ranked According to Percentage Success

RESULT/ SOURCE	NIF (%)	SPLC (%)	CN (%)	ATFL (%)
successful	43.56	52.53	48.44	64.36
unsuccessful	24.93	16.77	23.44	2.13
partially successful	10.99	17.72	14.06	33.51
other	20.52	12.98	14.06	0.00

Sources: Newsletter on Intellectual Freedom (1981-1990); *Student Press Law Center Report* (1981-1990); *Censorship News* (1981-1990); *Attacks on the Freedom to Learn* (1982-1990).

individual is seen as more severe. Because of this same concept of the severity of action taken against a person, incidents wherein a librarian or teacher has been harmed in some way or threatened with harm were also included in this group. These incidents did not always end with the material being banned, however. The *Newsletter on Intellectual Freedom* records six incidents (0.3% of all results recorded) wherein a librarian or some other responsible person was harmed or threatened, and the *Student Press Law Center Report* has recorded one incident (also 0.3% of all *SPLC* results recorded) (Table 4.12).

The second category represents the final outcome or a disposition that did not change the status of the item or access to it for its intended user or audience (Table 4.13). Although an objection has been made to such a work, an individual or governing body in authority or the courts have rejected the arguments against it, or the complaint has been withdrawn or ended in some other fashion. From an intellectual freedom point of view, this can be considered a positive outcome because the censorship attempt was unsuccessful.

The third group of result categories indicates that some compromise was made, or that restrictions on access exist without banning or expurgating the material. In several cases involving required or optional reading in classroom instruction, compromises such as moving the item from the required reading list to the optional reading list have been recorded. Other restrictions in this group include requiring parental permission, restricting use to an older age group, placing the item on a restricted shelf that requires an in-person request to obtain it, or delays or substitutes in use or access. From an intellectual freedom point of view, this can be considered a negative outcome because it is possible that such actions may deny access to materials to their intended user. A fourth group of categories includes cases where no discernible outcome has been recorded as of this research.

As Table 4.13 shows, for the ten-year period 1981-1990, the *Newsletter on Intellectual Freedom* reported 946 of 2,174 results (43.56%) as having successfully banned, removed, canceled, expurgated, or otherwise denied access to an expressive work. Similarly, the *Attacks on the Freedom to Learn* reported 121 of 188 outcomes (64.36%) with a successful challenge and *Censorship News* reported thirty-one of sixty-four (48.44%) as successful. The *Student Press Law Center Report*, because of its specialized focus, required a different set of result categories but also reported 166 out of 316 instances (52.53%) with a successful challenge. If the successful challenges are combined with those that formed a compromise position or were partially successful (see Table 4.13), from an intellectual freedom concern, the *NIF* indicates that fully 54.5% of the reported incidents (1,185 out of 2,174) had a negative outcome. Likewise the *ATFL* shows 97.87% (184 of 188) with a negative outcome, *Censorship News* 62.5% negative, and the *SPLC Report* 71.03% negative.

An examination of individual result categories also shows that in all four sources used in this research, the most frequent result is that the item has been banned or removed. The *NIF* recorded 393 of 2,174 (18.1% of the total) have been banned, as compared with the next most frequent result, that a complaint had been filed but no action had been taken at the time of the report (289 of 2,174, or 13.29% of the total). The "item banned" data is also prominent in the other three sources: *ATFL*--seventy-eight of 188 (41.49% of the total); *CN*--twenty-one of sixty-four (32.81% of the total); and *SPLC Report*--forty-two of 316 (13.29% of the total).

Table 4.12 also demonstrates the distribution of outcomes for each of the authoritative decision-making groups: review committees, school boards or library boards, and individual authorities. The *Newsletter on Intellectual Freedom* has the most significant data and it shows that review committees have recommended that the work be kept or not banned in 100 cases out of 169 review committee decisions (59.17%), but also recommended that the work be banned in thirty of the cases (17.75%) whereas thirty-nine cases received some form of restriction in their recommendation (23.1%).

School board/library board data in the *NIF* show a somewhat better picture. In 288 incidents, such boards have voted to keep or not ban such items, or 67.76% of the total school board/library board decisions. Only eighty-seven cases, or 20.47% of the total, report a school or library board voting to ban a book or other work. School or library boards apparently have less of a tendency to keep an item with restrictions (fifty out of 425 cases, or 11.76% of the total).

However, when individual authority data is reviewed, an entirely different picture emerges. Successful censorship attempts for those result categories attributed to an individual decision maker account for 688 of all incidents. This shows that an overwhelming number of outcomes made by individuals acting alone in an official capacity culminate in an act of censorship. Such individuals refused to ban or otherwise support books and other works in seventy-five dispositions or 3.45% of the total. This data indicates that governing boards tend to support access to materials and expressive works, but that individuals in authority will more often act to prohibit them in some way. This may be because many individuals in authority can act on their own without fear of a governing authority or to avoid a perceived threat from such bodies.

CENSORSHIP: WHO ARE THE ADVOCATES?

A new dimension to the compilation of censorship data from reporting sources was added to this study that has not been included in previous research. Whereas, other researchers have seen the importance of compiling statistics on who the censors are, this work sees the value in who the advocates for expressive work are as well. Some limiting factors have reduced the amount of data gathered, however. Not all reports in the four sources include statistics on advocates. Although the *Newsletter on Intellectual Freedom* identified forty-four categories of advocates, only 989 instances of advocate data have been recorded in the ten years' worth of issues (Table 4.14). This compares with 2,174 possible cases where advocate data could have been recorded. Furthermore, those reports with such information have often listed more than one category of advocate; therefore, the 989 instances represent even fewer distinct cases. Additionally, in establishing the criteria for defining an advocate for the purpose of this study, any aspect of the report merely quoting someone who appeared to be defending the book has not been considered for inclusion unless the report indicated that the individual has played a substantial role in its defense or acted in its behalf, beyond a newsworthy quote. Furthermore, individuals who are seen as natural advocates, for example, librarians for the defense of their own collection or teachers for the defense of their own assigned readings, were also not considered advocates unless they acted in some substantial way to protect or defend the item. In addition to these defining concepts, governing boards whose authority is to review or vote for or against an item, or courts whose job it is to interpret the law and the correctness of an action taken have also not been considered advocates if they merely exercised their authority, even though the board or the court may have ruled in favor of the item. Such actions are seen as their proper role, not an advocacy position. However, if the review committee or any of its members, a governing board or its members, or a court official acted in a substantial way to defend the item, then for these cases, they were considered an advocate.

As Table 4.14 indicates, the most frequent advocate mentioned in the *Newsletter on Intellectual Freedom* is a teacher, professor, or teacher union or professional association. Teachers have accounted for 139 of 989 recorded advocates, or 14.05% of all advocate data. Teachers play a significant role in the reports in *Censorship News* and the *Student Press Law Center Report*, accounting for 21.95% of all *CN* advocate data and 11.54% of all *SPLC Report* advocate data. No significant advocate data has been reported in *Attacks on the Freedom to Learn*. As Table 4.14 shows, the most frequent advocates are

Table 4.14 Advocates Listed in Censorship Attempts

ADVOCATE/SOURCE	NIF	SPLC	CN	ATFL
teacher, professor	138	9	8	6
citizen	114		4	1
ACLU	110	32	1	
student	100	7	9	3
parent	60	2	12	4
authors, agents, etc.	41		1	
state library association	35			
school board	34			
superintendent	31			
newspaper, staff	26	8	2	
publisher, printer, distributor	25			
labor union	25			
principal	22			
locally organized groups	21		2	2
arts, films council	18			
government official	13			
library board, librarian	13		1	
minister	13			
business, businessman	13			
school official	11		1	
National Coalition Against Censorship	9			
NAACP, civil rights groups	8	1		
professional	6	3		
U.S. Senator, Congressman	6			
city council	5			
American Library Association	5			
gay activists	5			
Center for Constitutional Rights	5			
Student Press Law Center	4	8		
civic club	4			
television station	4			
state senator, representative	3			
People for the American Way	3			
ethnic societies	3			
university official	3	4		
National Council of Teachers of English	3			
Planned Parenthood	2			
Action for Children's Television	2			
Moral Majority	1			
Jewish groups	1			
American Historical Association	1			
Reporter's Committee for Freedom of the Press	1			
celebrities	1			
student newspaper	2			
Society of Professional Journalists	1			

Table 4.14 (continued)

ADVOCATE/SOURCE	NIF	SPLC	CN	ATFL
Rutherford Institute		1		
subscriber		1		

Sources: Newsletter on Intellectual Freedom (1981-1990); *Student Press Law Center Report* (1981-1990); *Censorship News* (1981-1990); *Attacks on the Freedom to Learn*

individuals in the community where the censorship attempt takes place. Teachers, local citizens, students, parents, school board members, superintendents, and newspaper editors occupy the most frequent ranks of the *NIF* advocate data and nine of the next ten ranks of advocate data are local individuals as well.

Although national organizations do not play a significant role in advocacy, at least as indicated by this data, the American Civil Liberties Union (ACLU) is clearly an exception. It is the only national group that appears in three sets of the data. The ACLU is listed 110 times in the *Newsletter on Intellectual Freedom*, ranking third of all advocate categories and accounting for 11.12% of all the data (see Table 4.14). In the *SPLC Report*, it is first of all advocate groups, ranking even higher than the Student Press Law Center. The other known groups have much less frequency in the *NIF* with the National Coalition Against Censorship (9 instances or 1% of the data) and the National Association for the Advancement of Colored People (NAACP) the next most frequent. Only one of the ten categories of *Censorship News* advocate data is a nationally organized group (ACLU) or outside individuals (authors), but five of the twelve advocate categories recorded in the *Student Press Law Center Report* are nationally known groups or individuals based elsewhere than in the community. The data also appears to show that state library association intellectual freedom committees are often involved in the defense of challenged materials with thirty-six reports of advocacy in the *NIF* data (3.54% of the total).

5 Comparison of Sources: Past and Present

Chapter 4 demonstrated that a considerable body of data has been compiled on censorship attempts during the 1980s. Although the results compiled from the different categories of data and their analysis have value in and of themselves, some useful comparisons can be made with other sources. Chapter 4 made some comparisons of the data provided by each of the four reporting sources utilized by this research. Two other useful comparisons are viewed as worth including in this book. First, two major statistical studies of censorship attempts report similar information and provide a retrospective view of recent censorship history, L. B. Woods' *A Decade of Censorship in America* (1979) and Lee Burress' *The Battle of the Books* (1989). The methods used to gather data, the sources of information, and the time periods are somewhat different, but the results they provide are a window to the past that allows for gauging or comparing the data of the 1980s with historical censorship attempts. Second, the information from the four sources in this study is rich enough to review and compare the advantages and disadvantages of each of the four sources for statistical research on the censorship phenomena. Such comparisons are valuable to researchers of the future, to individuals who wish to gather current information on censorship challenges, and to intellectual freedom advocates.

Comparisons are not without their problems, however. For this research, there are too many factors that prohibit a perfect comparison, thus the same conclusions cannot necessarily be met. First, it must be remembered that these studies cover different time periods. Woods' study is for one decade, 1966-1975, which follows the same design as this work. Burress, however, covers a thirty-five year period, five years of which overlap with this study. That makes Woods' book somewhat easier for making such comparisons of a past decade to the one being examined. Although the years of data are different, the intent in making such comparisons is to gauge the transformation of censorship challenges over time, and to benchmark the data as much as possible

Second, the method for data gathering is different in each study. Again, the

Woods survey is very similar to the current one and matches the design closely, but it has gathered data from only one source and does not include all attributes included in this work. Burress utilized the results of numerous surveys and information he gathered during his career. Although this is substantially different from this book, the span of time is much greater and affords a more retrospective comparison. Furthermore, Burress reports censorship of materials, primarily books, from educational institutions, whereas censorship attempts from any institution reported are included in this research. However, each of these works permits the attributes to be categorized in the same manner and useful comparisons are possible.

CENSORED MATERIALS: PAST AND PRESENT

The targets of censorship have always been the primary concern of intellectual freedom advocates. It is the study of what has been censored that measures the rigors of censorious activities and the value structure that such activities attempt to impose on society. The defense of expressive rights requires an identification of what is being suppressed. This has been true for this research as well as the two historical studies analyzed in this chapter.

As shown in Table 5.1, Woods reports that the three most censored titles for 1966-1975 are *Catcher in the Rye*, (Table 5.1) *Soul on Ice*, and *Manchild in the Promised Land*. Burress also reports *Catcher in the Rye* as the most censored item during the thirty-five years of his statistical analysis, with *Go Ask Alice*, *Nineteen Eighty Four*, and *Grapes of Wrath* as experiencing almost the same level of objections. Of the twenty most frequent titles on both retrospective lists, nine are reported by both studies, although not in the same rank, with the exception of *Catcher in the Rye*. Of the twenty titles listed in Burress' book, four do not appear at all on Woods' lists: *Forever* (published during the last year of his research), *One Day in the Life of Ivan Denisovich*, *Johnny Got His Gun*, and *A Hero Ain't Nothing But a Sandwich*.

In the current study of the 1980s, the title list looks vastly different. Of the top twenty items, *Playboy* and *Penthouse* magazines far outweigh all other titles in frequency. Of the next eighteen items on the list, fourteen are books and six of these are written by Judy Blume. Blume's *Deenie* is the most censored book in the 1980s as measured by the *Newsletter on Intellectual Freedom* articles for the decade with *Forever* and *Then Again, Maybe I Won't* receiving almost as many challenges. There are no other authors known to have foregone a sustained, intensive attack on all works published as Judy Blume has during the 1980s. Some of the reports indicated that the complaint demanded that all books by Judy Blume be banned, indicating a strong value judgment against the author rather than a specific content-based objection.

The *NIF* list for the current decade does duplicate titles from the Woods and

Table 5.1 Twenty Most Censored Titles

NIF	#	ATFL	#	WOODS	#	BURRESS	#
1 Playboy	47	Catcher in the Rye	8	Catcher in the Rye	41	Catcher in the Rye	94
2 Penthouse	25	Impressions	6	Soul on Ice	20	Go Ask Alice	57
3 Deenie	18	The Chocolate War	5	Manchild in the Promised Land	15	Grapes of Wrath	28
4 Forever	17	Cujo	5	Go Ask Alice	14	Nineteen Eighty-Four	28
5 Then Again, Maybe I Won't	17	Go Ask Alice	5	Catch-22	10	Of Mice and Men	23
6 Adventures of Huckleberry Finn	16	Romeo and Juliet	5	Nudes (photos and art)	10	Manchild in the Promised Land	19
7 Of Mice and Men	15	Blubber	4	Grapes of Wrath	9	Our Bodies, Ourselves	19
8 Show Me!	15	Curses, Hexes, and Spells	4	Of Mice and Men	7	Adventures of Huckleberry Finn	16
9 Go Ask Alice	13	Forever	4	Slaughter-house Five	7	Forever	16
10 Catcher in the Rye	11	Of Mice and Men	4	To Kill A Mockingbird	7	One Flew Over the Cuckoo's Nest	15
11 Blubber	11	Deenie	3	Down These Mean Streets	6	The Learning Tree	14
12 Are You There, God? It's Me, Margaret	10	Halloween ABC	3	The Godfather	6	Slaughter-House Five	14

Table 5.1 (continued)

NIF	#	ATFL	#	WOODS	#	BURRESS	#
13 Doonesbury	10	I Am the Cheese	3	Inner City Mother Goose	6	One Day in the Life of Ivan Denisovich	13
14 Dungeons & Dragons	10	I Know Why the Caged Bird Sings	3	The Learning Tree	6	Brave New World	12
15 Hustler	10	Servants of the Devil	3	Lord of the Flies	6	My Darling, My, Hamburger	12
16 Playgirl	10	Sports Illustrated	3	Nigger	6	Black Boy	11
17 Last Temptation of Christ	9	Then Again, Maybe I Won't	3	Sylvester and the Magic Pebble	6	A Hero Ain't Nothing But a Sandwhich	10
18 Changing Bodies, Changing Lives	9	Adventures of Huckleberry Finn	2	Black Like Me	5	Johnny Got His Gun	10
19 The Chocolate War	9	Christine	2	Deliverance	5	Lord of the Flies	10
20 Our Bodies, Ourselves	9	The Color Purple	2	Flowers for Algernon	5	To Kill a Mockingbird	10

Sources: *Newsletter on Intellectual Freedom* (1981-1990); *Attacks on the Freedom to Learn* (1982-1990);   Woods (1979); Burress (1989).

Burress studies but some prominent titles from these previous studies, either fail to appear in the data or are of little frequency. Of the twenty most frequently censored books in 1966-1975, seven do not appear in any report in the *NIF* for the 1980s:

Catch 22, by Joseph Heller
Down These Mean Streets, by Walt Pirie
Inner City Mother Goose
Nigger, by Dick Gregory
Sylvester and the Magic Pebble, by William Steig
Black Like Me, by John Griffin
Deliverance, by James Dickey

Additionally, *Soul on Ice*, *The Godfather*, and *The Learning Tree* only appear once (see Appendix A). All of these titles seem to have either entered the mainstream or are no longer frequently read books. Other titles from Woods' research of note, due to at least a relatively high frequency of censorship in his study, include *The Exorcist*, *Little Black Sambo*, and the film *Birth of a Nation*. These titles also do not appear in the most recent data. The *Adventures of Huckleberry Finn* and *Our Bodies, Ourselves* rank high on Woods' list and in the current *NIF*, but with greater frequency in the 1980s. Table 5.1 also shows that *Go Ask Alice* and *Of Mice and Men* are still challenged in a significant way.

The Burress list also has quite similar patterns. A major difference between Burress and Woods is that Judy Blume books, especially *Forever*, appear in his data in a prominent way. Burress' study covers up to 1985 and this accounts for that difference. Nine of the other Burress titles with substantial frequency are also on the top of Woods' list and both found *Catcher in the Rye* to be the most censored title. Four other titles, *Brave New World*, *Black Boy*, *My Darling, My Hamburger*, and *One Flew Over the Cuckoo's Nest* appear on both retrospective lists, although ranked much higher by Burress. Burress also found five titles with a significant number of censorship attempts that Woods did not find in his 1966-1975 data:

Forever, by Judy Blume
A Hero Ain't Nothing But a Sandwich, by Alice Childress
Johnny Got His Gun, by Dalton Trumbo
One Day in the Life of Ivan Denisovich, by Aleksandr Solzhenitsyn
Our Bodies, Ourselves, by Boston Women's Health Cooperative

When the Burress titles are compared with those found in the *NIF* for 1981-1990, five appear on the top twenty list of both:

Forever, by Judy Blume
Adventures of Huckleberry Finn, by Mark Twain
Go Ask Alice, Anonymous
Catcher in the Rye, by J.D. Salinger
Our Bodies, Ourselves, by Boston Women's Health Cooperative

One of the most important facts in this analysis is that *Catcher in the Rye* and *Go Ask Alice* are the only titles that remain consistently within the twenty most frequent ranks throughout all three research reports.

This study also developed a complete list of titles challenged as reported in the two other book censorship reporting sources, the *Attacks on the Freedom to Learn* (see Table 5.1) and *Censorship News*. The *ATFL* has the most significant data of the two. The titles it has found challenged from 1981-1990 are similar to the *NIF* list of titles for the same time period. Four Judy Blume books, *Blubber*, *Deenie*, *Forever* and *Then Again, Maybe I Won't* are among the twenty most censored. Additionally, the *ATFL* reports significant challenges against

Robert Cormier's *The Chocolate War* and frequent attempts against Cormier's *I Am the Cheese*, as does the *NIF*. *The Chocolate War* appears on Burress' list but not Woods', although it was published in 1974. Like Burress and Woods, the *ATFL* found *Catcher in the Rye* with the most censorship attempts, not Blume's *Deenie*. As mentioned earlier, both *Catcher in the Rye* and *Go Ask Alice* are the only titles that remain constant on all lists, including the *ATFL*.

The *Censorship News* list of censored titles for 1981-1990 lacks sufficient data to make similar comparisons and is not included in Table 5.1. However, it also points to the strong challenges to Judy Blume books, including *Forever, Blubber, Deenie, Then Again, Maybe I Won't*, and *Are You There God? It's Me, Margaret. Catcher in the Rye, The Chocolate War*, and *Brave New World* also appear on its list, but not *Go Ask Alice*. The titles from the *Student Press Law Center Report* do not demonstrate any significant challenges to any one title. Furthermore, most student presses are not recognizable nor have they received any national recognition. A complete list of these titles is included in Appendix.

YEARLY TOTALS OF CENSORSHIP: PAST AND PRESENT

Since this study has gathered data for each year of the decade 1981-1990, trends in the total number of censorship attempts can be compared to L. B. Woods' 1966-1975 statistics (see Table 5.2). Burress' work, however, covers a thirty-five-year period, but does not compile totals by year. The yearly censorship challenges for 1966-1975, as reported by Woods, are few in total number for the first four years of that time period. However, significant increases begin in 1970, and are particularly substantial for the last three years Woods studied, rising from a low of forty-three for the entire year of 1966 to a high of 563 in 1975. The current data for censorship attempts reported in the *NIF* for the decade 1981-1990 shows relatively steady numbers of challenges throughout most of the decade. Only the first year, 1981, rises above 300 (365 total), with the next six years averaging approximately 252 per year. Beginning in 1988, the level of censorship reported begins to decline to totals similar to the first part of the decade studied by Woods. However, the total number of censorship attempts for the two decades of *NIF* data is almost the same: 2,178 for Woods 1966-1975 study and 2,174 for this current research, a difference of four attempts. As mentioned earlier, the fervor of the conservatives immediately after the Reagan election appears to have been reflected in the strength of the attacks in the early part of the decade.

Data from the *Attacks on the Freedom to Learn, Censorship News*, and *SPLC Report* are not comparable in volume to make similar comparisons (see Table 5.2), however, the *ATFL* is better for gauging trends in total censorship attempts. There are only nine years of data, but the first five of those years have reported an average of almost thirty attempts each year. During the next four years, the

Table 5.2   Total Number of Censorship Attempts per Year

YEAR	NIF	CN	ATFL	SPLC	YEAR	WOODS
1981	365	5	0	7	1966	43
1982	259	0	17	9	1967	91
1983	233	6	33	12	1968	65
1984	290	5	36	23	1969	83
1985	232	8	25	24	1970	223
1986	230	5	33	29	1971	248
1987	270	4	56	28	1972	187
1988	167	1	34	33	1973	294
1989	77	3	62	37	1974	381
1990	51	3	48	31	1975	563

Sources: Newsletter on Intellectual Freedom (1981-1990); *Censorship News* (1981-1990); *Attacks on the Freedom to Learn* (1982-1990); *Student Press Law Center Report* (1981-1990); Woods(1979).

reports have grown, more than doubling that average in 1989 (sixty-two attempts). Since the *ATFL* is an annual that reports a selective sample of the censorship challenges reported to the People for the American Way, these statistics could be a function of better reporting and coverage over the life of this periodical rather than a trend in total censorship attempts.

CENSORED FORMATS: PAST AND PRESENT

In 1979, Woods reported that for the 1966-1975 decade, books were the target of censorship 55% of the time, with textbooks challenged 13.7% (see Table 5.3). Books remain the most challenged format throughout the current study, with 40.98% of all items included in the *NIF* for 1981-1990, 65.55% of all material listed in the *ATFL* and 65.85% of all items reported by *Censorship News*. The *NIF* data may indicate that other formats are being censored more than in the past, however. Lee Burress did not compile any specific data on format. More than 90% of his data appears to be books and textbooks. The variations in the findings of this work and that of Woods arise out of the remaining formats. Woods has found textbooks to be the second most challenged format with newspapers and speakers relatively close in total number of attempts. Magazines do not show a significant impact in his data (3.3% of the total). In the current study, the *ATFL* and *Censorship News* also do not show magazines as a threatened format (Table 5.3). *Censorship News* does not report any censored periodical titles and *ATFL* shows only 2.72% of the data as censored magazine titles. However, the *Newsletter on Intellectual Freedom* has more substantial data and is comparable to Woods' research. It indicates that magazine censorship is a serious problem, accounting for 9.43% of the 1981-1990 data.

Textbooks (8.19%), film (8.00%), and student newspapers (5.84%) are also heavily censored materials as reported by the *NIF* for this time period. The *Student Press Law Center Report* has the most significant data on censored student press formats, and this data indicates that of all the possible types of student publications, the official school newspaper is the most censored form (See Table 5.3).

Table 5.3 Number of Challenges According to Format

FORMAT/ SOURCE	NIF	CN	ATFL	SPLC	WO
advertisement	27	2	1		
alternative press				22	
art	83				13
art magazine				3	
book	891	27	217		1197
comic	32				1
dance	4				
document	8				2
exhibit	21		23		3
film	174	2			50
game	13			1	
literary magazine				6	
magazine	205		9		72
music	41				16
newspaper	44				188
other	93		46	25	202
play	68		20		17
radio	16				4
speech	70		3	2	117
student newspaper	127	1		169	
student press	24	2			2
television	55				2
textbook	178	7	11		300
yearbook				17	

Sources: Newsletter on Intellectual Freedom (1981-1990); *Censorship News* (1981-1990); *Attacks on the Freedom to Learn* (1982-1990); *Student Press Law Center Report* (1981-1990); Woods (1979).

WHERE CENSORSHIP OCCURS: PAST AND PRESENT

The landscape of censorship appears to have changed from that of 1966-1975 when the present study is compared to that of L. B. Woods and to the book by

Burress (see Table 5.4). As with Woods' work, it has been assumed that there should be a one-to-one correlation of total censorship attempts with population. In other words, instead of comparing raw totals for each state, it is necessary to gauge their impact relative to total population or where each state ranks in population. A state ranked tenth in population should, for example, rank approximately tenth in total censorship attempts.

Table 5.4 Number of Censorship Attempts According to State

STATE/ SOURCE	NIF	CN	ATFL	SPLC	WO	BU
Alabama	41	5	12	2	11	10
Alaska	2	1	2		4	3
Arizona	26		11	2	6	44
Arkansas	27		1		4	14
California	187	2	30	32	123	60
Colorado	71		10	6	14	10
Connecticut	24		4	2	21	10
Delaware	7		1		3	
District of Columbia	68			4	17	
Florida	163	2	20	9	40	14
Georgia	44		5	1	14	4
Hawaii			1	1		3
Idaho	13		2	1	3	5
Illinois	100	4	3	13	48	46
Indiana	28		4	8	15	45
Iowa	50	2	7	4	20	20
Kansas	26	1	5	2	10	12
Kentucky	30	1	2	2	8	6
Louisiana	37	2	4	4	10	79
Maine	19	1	3	4	3	15
Maryland	52		8	7	47	17
Massachusetts	51		1	8	22	14
Michigan	73	1	17	10	47	28
Minnesota	59	6	3	2	12	17
Mississippi	11		3		5	7
Missouri	38	1	8	4	12	20
Montana	16			3	5	4
Nebraska	36		3	2	3	10
Nevada	11		3		1	
New Hampshire	13		2	1	9	5
New Jersey	28	1	4	10	37	14
New Mexico	17	1	2	2	5	5
New York	103	2	10	20	70	77
North Carolina	38	1	5	3	14	15
North Dakota	10		3		2	4

Table 5.4 (continued)

STATE/SOURCE	NIF	CN	ATFL	SPLC	WO	BU
Ohio	56		13	5	31	83
Oklahoma	22	1	7	5	8	13
Oregon	45		15		21	11
Pennsylvania	76		16	11	29	46
Rhode Island	16		1	1	18	1
South Carolina	11	1	5	3	5	14
South Dakota	14		5	2		6
Tennessee	24		6		11	21
Texas	67	2	17	12	35	62
Utah	9		1	1	2	3
Vermont	11		3		5	6
Virginia	67	1	12	10	34	19
Washington	78	2	18	3	7	22
West Virginia	18		8	2	3	3
Wisconsin	104		10		27	125
Wyoming	36		6	1	4	5

Sources: Newsletter on Intellectual Freedom (1981-1990); *Censorship News* (1981-1990); *Attacks on the Freedom to Learn* (1982-1990); *Student Press Law Center Report* (1981-1990); Woods (1979); Burress (1989).

This analysis was made from a comparison of statistics calculated from the population figures from the *U.S. Statistical Abstract.* As mentioned earlier, using an index of percentage of censorship total to percent of population closely correlates to the use of per capita figures. Since Woods used the former method, a comparison of Woods' 1966-1975 report with the results of data from the *NIF* of 1981-1990 can be more readily made and this shows there are some similarities and some differences where the most frequent censorship attempts took place:

1966-1975	1981-1990
1. District of Columbia	1. District of Columbia
2. Rhode Island	2. Wyoming
3. Vermont	3. Nebraska
4. Maryland	4. Colorado
5. New Hampshire	5. Wisconsin
6. Oregon	6. South Dakota
7. Wyoming	7. Montana
8. Alaska	8. Vermont
9. Montana	9. Iowa
10. Virginia	10. Rhode Island and Washington

Of the two studies, four states (the District of Columbia, Wyoming, Montana, and Vermont) are found within these ten ranks on both lists. On the 1981-1990 list, three of the states with the highest indexing are on the East Coast. The remaining eight are either farm-belt Midwestern states or Western states (see

Table 4.4 for regional division) whereas Woods' data shows three New England, two Mid-Atlantic, one Southern, and three Western states. A look at the states ranked eleven through twenty, also indicates that the censorship of the most recent decade comes primarily from the Western and farm-belt Midwestern states. Four of the next ten highest indexed states of the 1980s are located in these two geographic areas, but with three in this grouping from New England and two in the South (see Table 5.3). Woods' results show a greater variation among the regions for the states with the highest censorship than in this current study.

The level of censorship in the states as measured by Burress over a thirty-five year period produces slightly different results but still indicates a strong climate of censorship in the Western and farm belt Midwestern states (see Table 5.5). There is a difficulty in producing an indexed ranking of Burress' data because this time period covered has experienced wide-ranging changes in population of the states. Tests of population figures from several other years, however, yields very few differences in placing states in a ranked list such as this. Indexing the level of censorship with population figures of the mid-1980s yields eight states in the Midwestern farm belt in the twenty states with the most censorship, and six states in the West, including the Pacific Northwest. The difference of Burress' study from that of Woods and the current study is the wide variation in the states he reports, even within the Western and Midwestern regions (see Table 5.5).

Table 5.5 Comparison of Level of Censorship by State Indexed by Population (C = percentage of censorship, P = percentage of population)

	WOODS				BURRESS				SPLC, 1981-1990				NIF, 1981-1990		
ST	Index C/P	C(%)	P(%)	ST	Index C/P	C(%)	P(%)	ST	Index C/P	C(%)	P(%)	ST	IndexCP	C(%)	P(%)
DC	6.33	1.90	0.30	WI	5.75	11.61	2.02	DC	6.85	1.78	.26	DC	13.08	3.13	0.24
RI	5.00	2.00	0.40	LA	3.88	7.34	1.89	MT	3.80	1.33	.35	WY	9.22	1.66	0.18
VT	3.00	0.60	0.20	AZ	3.15	4.09	1.30	ME	3.63	1.78	.49	NE	2.63	1.66	0.63
MD	2.74	5.20	1.90	ME	2.84	13.9	0.49	SD	2.96	.89	.30	CO	2.48	3.27	1.32
NH	2.50	1.00	0.40	VT	2.43	0.56	0.23	WY	2.00	.44	.22	WI	2.44	4.65	1.97
OR	2.09	2.30	1.10	WY	2.09	0.46	0.22	CO	1.98	2.67	1.35	SD	2.32	0.73	0.28
WY	2.00	0.40	0.20	SD	1.87	0.56	0.30	VA	1.86	4.44	2.39	MT	2.31	0.50	0.32
AK	2.00	0.40	0.20	IN	1.79	4.18	2.33	MD	1.69	3.11	1.84	VT	2.22	0.64	0.23
MT	2.00	0.60	0.30	OH	1.69	7.71	4.57	OK	1.59	2.22	1.40	IA	2.06	2.16	1.12
VA	1.65	3.80	2.30	IA	1.50	1.86	1.24	IN	1.53	3.56	2.33	RI	1.85	3.55	0.40
IA	1.57	2.20	1.40	NE	1.37	0.93	0.68	NM	1.48	.89	.60	WA	1.85	2.07	1.96
CT	1.53	2.30	1.50	AK	1.33	0.28	0.21	IO	1.45	1.72	1.23	OR	1.81	0.73	1.14
WI	1.43	3.00	2.10	AR	1.31	1.30	0.99	NJ	1.40	4.44	3.18	ME	1.80	0.46	0.49
CO	1.36	1.50	1.10	ND	1.26	0.37	0.29	CA	1.31	14.22	10.85	ND	1.77	2.72	0.26
CA	1.35	13.50	10.00	NH	1.12	0.46	0.41	NE	1.31	.89	.68	MN	1.55	7.42	1.76
MI	1.26	5.40	4.30	WA	1.11	2.04	1.83	IL	1.18	5.78	4.88	ID	1.50	0.60	0.40
NM	1.20	0.60	0.50	ID	1.07	0.46	0.43	NY	1.18	8.89	7.51	FL	1.43	1.99	5.20
FL	1.18	4.50	3.80	KS	1.07	1.11	1.04	MI	1.16	4.44	3.84	NH	1.33	0.60	0.46
NJ	1.17	4.10	3.50	MT	1.06	0.37	0.35	NH	1.07	.44	.41	NM	1.28	0.78	0.61
DE	1.00	0.30	0.30	TN	0.98	1.95	2.00	RI	1.07	.44	.41	AR	1.26	2.39	0.95

Sources: Woods (1979); Burress (1989); *Newsletter on Intellectual Freedom* (1981-1990).

This same analysis can be made from the data of the *Student Press Law Center Report* that gives a picture of where student press censorship is particularly heavy, though the statistics are not as substantial as the *NIF*. A pattern of censorship of the student press in the farm-belt and Western states is also apparent, although not as clearly as materials censorship. Eight states from these geographic regions are among the twenty most censorious, based on the indexed data from the *SPLC Report,* with general censorship sources. The District of Columbia has the highest rates of student press censorship in relation to its population.

This same pattern of a heavy censorship climate in the farm belt Midwest and the West, especially the Pacific Northwest, is shown by the data from the *Attacks on the Freedom to Learn* (Table 5.4). Seven Midwestern and six Western states have the most frequent censorship attempts in relationship to population as recorded by the *ATFL* from 1981-1990. *Censorship News* has recorded very few attempts, with only thirteen states all total with any challenges listed. In total numbers, only Minnesota, Illinois, and Alabama have more than two recorded incidents reported in this periodical.

INSTITUTIONS WHERE CENSORSHIP OCCURS: PAST AND PRESENT

A comparison of institutional censorship can also be made from the statistics of the current study and L. B. Woods' *A Decade of Censorship in America* (see Table 5.6). Lee Burress' book, *Battle of the Books,* however has not recorded the institutions affected by censorship challenges. All sources of data, that is, the four censorship periodicals used for this study and L. B. Woods' book, show that censorship attempts occur more often at the high school level, including textbook and library book censorship, than in any other institution. Woods reports 386 attempts in high schools (42.27% of all educational institutions). This study shows that for all institutions, the four reporting sources have recorded the following data on high school censorship attempts:

NIF: 585 of 2233 (26.20%)
ATFL: 139 of 506 (27.47%)
CN: 11 of 42 (26.19%)
SPLC: 115 of 234 (49.15%)

When only educational institutions are factored, high school censorship plays an even greater role:

NIF: 585 of 1579 (37.05%)
ATFL: 139 of 311 (44.69%)
CN: 11 of 38 (28.95%)

Table 5.6 Number of Censorship Challenges by Institution

INSTITUTION	NIF	CN	ATFL	SPLC	WOODS
high school	424	10	98	115	386
university, college	204			106	236
public library	185	1	7		110
high school library	161	1	41		
elementary library	154	7	42		
school	133		4	1	64
retail outlet	133	1			
elementary school	80		30		40
junior high library	74	2	49		
school library	73	5	29		
junior high school	70	6	36	3	77
tv station, program	68				
state committee, state library	49		3		
theater	48		1		
museums, centers, exhibits	47				
public forum	46				
newspaper publisher	37	1			
prison	22	1			
radio station, program	21		1		
church	21		1		
book publisher, printer	20				
stage performance	20				
federal government	17				
film company, producer	17				
magazine publisher, printer	16				
none given	15	1	3		
music industry, producer	15		95		
advertising industry	14		11		
school district	13	4	5		
film festival	13		10		
scouts, youth groups	6		12		
labor union	2		23		
library of congress	2				
public schools	2	3			
media center	2				
community college, technical school				8	
other				1	

Sources: Newsletter on Intellectual Freedom (1981-1985); *Censorship News* (1981-1990); *Attacks on the Freedom to Learn* (1982-1990); *Student Press Law Center* (1981-1990); Woods (1979).

SPLC: 115 of 233 (49.35%)

Although these statistics closely parallel Woods' in percentages, there appears to be a more diversified impact across all institutions, both for educational and non-educational organizations in the 1980s data. Only public library and college challenges produced more than 10% of the total educational censorship attempts in 1966-1975. The current study shows that each educational organization accounts for almost 10% of the total, except junior high schools and junior high libraries (see Figures 4.3 [a-d]).

Woods mentions that data were collected on noneducational institutions, however, he does not report on these results extensively. During the 1981-1990 decade, the *Newsletter on Intellectual Freedom* shows that retail outlets are the target of the censor more often than any other noneducational institution (Table 5.6). The *Attacks on the Freedom to Learn*, however, fails to record any retail outlet censorship but finds the Music Industry to be attacked the most of any noneducational institution and the second most of all institutions. *Censorship News* reported only two incidents in non-educational institutions, one in a prison and one in a retail outlet (Table 5.6), while the *SPLC Report* indicates all but one incident has occurred in an educational setting.

THE COMPLAINANTS: PAST AND PRESENT

Some of the richest data of all the censorship sources, past and present, regards the individuals and groups who challenge expressive works (see Table 5.7). The most telling story is that every source of this research except the *Student Press Law Center Report* found that "parents" are the number one complainant, often accounting for a substantial amount of the total number of complainants recorded. Each source has reported the following data on parental complaints:

Woods: 248 (24.9% of all sources, but Citizens were included in the data)
Burress: 763 of 1,472 (51.83%)
NIF (1981-1990): 618 of 2,847 (21.7%)
ATFL (1981-1990): 123 of 478 (25.73%)
CN (1981-1990): 9 of 47 (19.15%)
SPLC (1981-1990): 3 of 256 (1.17%)

The findings of the three general censorship periodicals used in this study closely resemble the data reported by Woods in 1979. Burress indicates a much greater level of parental involvement. This can be attributed to the span of time or to his concentration in educational settings where parents have a more vested interest. The *Student Press Law Center Report*, having a specialized focus on the student press, appears to indicate that censorship emanates from school authorities and their need to control the student press rather than content objections by parents

Table 5.7   Complainants Listed in Censorship Attempts

COMPLAINANT/SOURCE	NIF	CN	ATFL	SPLC	WO	BU
parent	611	9	123	3	242	763
citizen	224	2	28	6		82
minister	220	4	7	1	32	66
principal	209	1	6	72		95
various organized groups	149	4	70		26	19
school board	135	8	1	6	144	65
government official	103		4		102	
student	103		2	14	28	77
university official	101		3	54		
superintendent	74	1				42
law enforcement official	69				23	
teacher, professor	65	3	1	13	26	152
city council, county commissioner	62					2
businesses	51		1		1	
librarian	38	3	40		25	71
TV station officials	34				2	
Eagle Forum	33	4				
newspaper, editor, staff	32		3		3	
state government official	27		2	3		
art museum, music hall, exhibit officials	25		2			
school personnel	25	1	9		2	
radio station officials	23					
Moral Majority	22		1	3		
Citizens for Excellence in Education	20		7			
American Family Association	19		2			
publisher, printer, distributor	19			1	6	
prison official	18	1				
ethnic groups	17		1		1	
library board	17		3			
Christian Broadcasting Network	16					
NAACP	15			8	5	
none given	15	2	11	2	21	
state board, state library	15					
U.S. Senator/ Congressman	15		16			
parents groups (PTA, PTO)	14		12		6	2
Anti-Defamation League	13		3			3
Citizens for Decency Through Law	12		1		3	
mayor, city manager	12					
National Organization For Women	12		3			2
Catholic League for Religious and Civil Rights	11		2			
professional	11		14			
Concerned Women for America	10		6			
feminists	10		1	1		
library staffer	10		1			
anti-abortion groups	8		38			

Table 5.7 (continued)

COMPLAIANT/SOURCE	NIF	CN	ATFL	SPLC	WO	BU
arts council	8		1			
Profamily Forum	8					
labor union	6					
Morality in Media	6		1			
American Society of Atheists	5					
celebrity	5					
National Coalition Against Pornography	5		9			
Educational Research Analysts	4		7			
gay activists	4		1			
Women Against Pornography	4		1			
Accuracy in Media/ Academia	3		6			
Church of Scientology	3		7			
Motion Picture Association of America	3		1			
National Coalition on Television Violence	3					
advertiser	2		7	2		
Focus on the Family	2		2			
youth groups or scouts officials	2		1			
Klu Klux Klan	1					
faculty advisor				7		
named individual				2		
Parent's Music Resource Center				1		
school alumnus				1	1	
school official		4	17	26	241	9
student government				16		
student paper, editor, staff				6		
Daughters of the American Revolution					2	
Gablers						10
Georgia Baptist Convention					1	
John Birch Society					7	2
Knights of Columbus					1	
Lions Club					1	
other					15	
review committee						2
state education official						7
Students for a Democratic Society					1	
Veterans of Foreign Wars					1	
Western Poverty Law Center					1	
Young Republicans Club					1	

Sources: Newsletter on Intellectual Freedom (1981-1990); *Censorship News* (1981-1990); *Attacks on the Freedom to Learn* (1982-1990); *Student Press Law Center Report* (1981-1990); Woods (1979); Burress (1989).

objections by parents or others.

As the censorship incidents have been compiled, both individuals by category and organized groups by group name have arisen out of the data (Table 5.7). L. B. Woods and Lee Burress also discovered that organized groups--local, grass roots, and nationally known associations--constitute a portion of the statistics on censorship sources. However, compared to the four periodicals examined for this research, both Woods and Burress report a limited impact by groups, especially by nationally known organizations (Table 5.8). Woods reported thirty-three incidents, of a total 912 (3.62%), originating with a committee or group outside educational institutions, with the John Birch Society topping the list with seven attempts. Likewise, Burress reported twenty incidents (of 1472 or 1.36%) attributed to known, nationally affiliated committees or groups, and ninenteen to locally organized groups, 1.29% of the total. The Gablers are the most frequent organization in Burress' data, with the Anti-Defamation League second in frequency. However, as mentioned in Chapter 4, twenty-three well-known organizations have been identified in the *NIF* data for 1981-1990, which account for 229 attempts or 8.19% of all recorded incidents (see Table 5.8). Only the NAACP remains constant in Woods, Burress, and the current *NIF* data, and only the Anti-Defamation League is listed in addition to this in the Burress data as well as the current statistics. This indicates that the face of censorship has changed and is more group oriented. The other three sources utilized for this research also approximate the level of group involvement that the *NIF* has shown (see Table 5.8). The *Attacks on the Freedom to Learn* has the best data in this regard, reporting seventy of 478 incidents (14.85%) attributed to a nationally affiliated organization, with the PTA creating the most attempts, twenty-one of the seventy-one. Though the John Birch Society, listed by Woods as the most censorious group, is also not mentioned by the *ATFL*, or any other current source studied, the *Attacks* has found censorship challenges by the PTA (twelve), the Gablers (seven) and Citizens for Decency through Law (one), which the most recent *NIF* issues have not reported. *Censorship News* also reports one organization, the Eagle Forum, with four of forty-seven attempts, or 8.5% of its data, and the *SPLC Report* has found three national groups, NAACP, Moral Majority, and the Parent's Music Resource Center, that have filed censorship complaints (Table 5.8).

This comparison demonstrates that censorship is growing toward more involvement by organized individuals. These groups are also overwhelmingly conservative in their orientation (see Chapter 4 analysis). In addition to the nationally recognized groups, locally organized or grass roots organizations also account for a greater number of the complainants in the current study than that reported by Woods and Burress (Table 5.8). Although *Censorship News* and the *Student Press Law Center Report* do not report any incidents of complaints from a local group, the *NIF* for the most recent decade found 149 incidents of 2,818 complainants (5.29%) attributed to a local, grassroots committee and the *Attacks*

Table 5.8 Number of Censorship Attempts Made by Organized Groups According to Political Orientation (PO; c = conservative, l = liberal, u = unknown)

GROUP/ SOURCE	PO	NIF	SPLC	CN	ATFL	WO	BU
Eagle Forum	c	33		4			
Moral Majority	c	22	3		1		
Citizens for Excellence in Education	c	20			7		
American Family Association	c	20			2		
Christian Broadcasting Network	c	15					
Citizens for Decency Through Law	c	12			1	3	
Catholic League for Religious and Civil Rights	c	11			2		
Concerned Women for America	c	10			6		
Profamily Forum	c	8					
Morality in Media	c	6			1		
National Coalition Against Pornography	c	5			9		
Women Against Pornography	c	4			1		
Educational Research Analysts	c	4			7		
Accuracy in Media/ Academia	c	3			6		
Focus on the Family	c	2			2		
Klu Klux Klan	c	1					
Daughters of the American Revolution	c					2	
John Birch Society	c					7	2
Young Republicans Club	c					1	
Gablers	c						10
N.A.A.C.P.	l	14	8			5	1
Anti-Defamation League	l	13			3		3
National Organization for Women	l	12			3		2
American Society of Atheists	l	5					
Students for a Democratic Society	l					1	
National Coalition on Television Violence	u	3					
Motion Picture Association of America	u	3			1		
Church of Scientology	u	3			7		
Parents Music Resource Center	u		1				
Georgia Baptist Convention	u					1	
Knights of Columbus	u					1	
Lions Club	u					1	
Veterans of Foreign Wars	u					1	
Western Poverty Law Center	u						
locally organized groups	u	149		4	70	26	19

Sources: Newsletter on Intellectual Freedom (1981-1990); *Student Press Law Center Report* (1981-1990); *Censorship News* (1981-1990); *Attacks on the Freedom to Learn* (1982-1990); Woods (1979); Burress (1989).

on the Freedom to Learn reported seventy of 478 complainants are locally based groups (14.64%). This compares to Woods who discovered only 1.86% of all attempts to have originated with a community pressure group and Burress who found an even smaller percentage of local group censorship (Table 5.8).

The frequency rankings for individuals by category vary from source to source. As mentioned earlier, "parents," categorically, are consistently the number one complainant in all but the *Student Press Law Center Report*. A comparison of the most frequent complainant categories for all six sources listed in Table 5.7 demonstrates that ten categories are consistently ranked as the most frequent complainants: Parent, Minister, Principal, Citizen, Local Groups, School Board, Student, Superintendent, and Librarian and Teacher. These ten categories are individuals who are either directly affiliated with a school, such as a teacher, student, principal, and school board, or who appear to have a close relationship or vested interest in the school: (1) parents who speak for their children who attend school, (2) ministers who are part of the community's extended family, and (3) citizens and local citizens' groups who pay taxes to the school or who may have children or grandchildren in attendance. A few exceptions to this observation exist in all six sources, but somewhat more so for Burress' study, Woods' research on the 1966-1975 *NIF*, and the current *NIF* (1981-1990) data. Both the 1966-1975 *NIF* issues and the 1981-1990 *NIF* issues give a much more relative importance to government and law enforcement sources of censorship than Burress and the other periodicals. But the emphasis on school connected individuals remains constant in all six sources.

OBJECTIONS MADE: PAST AND PRESENT

All six of the sources of censorship data have compiled data on the reasons given for the objection to the expressive work. Table 5.9 provides a comparison of the six publications and the statistics on objections. The *Student Press Law Center Report* is a specialized source, however. Its data reflects the concern for control of the student press, which is not as readily evident in the majority of data of the other five sources. Two categories--too critical of the school and --too negative of an image of the school, combined, account for almost 20 percent of all the reasons given in this title. Two other categories-libelous and inappropri-ate-, also may reflect more control issues than content-based objections, and these two categories represent another 12.5 percent of the data. However, the remaining six of the top categories are similar to the data in the other five sources. When the most frequent reasons are compared in all six sources, four of them appear at the top or within ten rankings in at least five or more of the six sets of research data: (1) Sexual Content--all six sources, (2) Profanity-five of the six, (3) Obscene or Pornographic--five of the six, and (4) Anti-Christian or Religious Objections--five of six. The predominance of sexually themed, content-based

Table 5.9   Reasons Given in Censorship Attempts

REASON/ SOURCE	NIF	CN	ATFL	SPLC	WO	BU
sexual content-based	533	6	41	22	320	139
profane	361	15	49	8	505	137
obscene	257	3	8	10	136	169
anti-religious, anti-Christian, sacreligious	136	6	20	6	52	64
occult, witchcraft, devil worship	133		36	2	20	
nudity, revealing clothing	121		5	8	15	
inappropriate	116	4	11	13	100	
homosexuality	82	1	6	10	19	
violence	72		11		49	11
none given	64	7	7		307	
racist	64		14	21	41	92
abortion	59	1	2	8	8	17
too critical of school	55			63	1	39
ridicules individuals or groups; ethnic slurs	54		14	8	2	
too critical of government	52					
violation of law or regulation	52			5		
drugs	49		1	5	14	25
immoral; lack of value	49	6	5	4	52	35
political tone	46		15		11	144
Secular Humanist, New Age	43		9		9	
inaccurate, misleading, poor grammar	43	1	1	17	12	23
anti-family, anti-family values	42	3	38		4	
causes disorder, fights, security problems	40		14	10	1	
sexist	39		1	8		
controversial	35	3	6		21	
disrespectful to police or authority; fosters disrespect	35	4	75	1	2	
violence against women	34		4	3	1	
too negative	33		7		13	
promotes a religion, violates separation of church and state	31		10	5	8	
too liberal	29	4	2	3	5	
anti-American	27	1	3	1	13	
anti-Semitic	26	1		2	6	
Marxist, communist, socialist	25		3		16	
contraceptives	22	1	3	11	2	
suicide	20		4	1		
feminist	20	3	5			
not approved; violates time, space regulations	19		3	5	2	24
libelous	17			26		
promotes evolution; does not promote creation	15		1		8	

Table 5.9 (continued)

REASON/SOURCE	NIF	CN	ATFL	SPLC	WO	BU
offensive to named individual	14		2			
anti-business; anti-wealthy	14			1		
alcohol	13		7	3	1	
violates privacy, individual rights	9		1	3	1	
anti-nuclear power, anti-war, anti-military	7	1		1	2	21
copyright, trademark infringement	7			2		
A.I.D.S.	6		3	3		
prostitution	3		1		6	
violates fair trial	3		2			
flag desecration	3		1			
too conservative	1		1	2		
violation of free speech	1		3			
too critical of labor union	1					
too critical of student government				6		
other				5		136
violation of school policy				4		
unsigned editorial				4		
disagreement with subject matter				2		

Sources: Newsletter on Intellectual Freedom (1981-1990); *Censorship News* (1981-1990); *Attacks on the Freedom to Learn* (1982-1990); *Student Press Law Center Report* (1981-1990); Woods (1979); Burress (1989).

are examined, particularly the next ten most frequent reasons, sexual themes continue to account for substantial amounts of the data in all six sources, with such complaints as "homosexuality," "immoral," "nudity," and "contraceptives" listed prominently on these lists (Table 5.9).

The remaining reasons that occur most frequently (within twenty ranks on any list) do not form any recognizable pattern. Woods reports more concern about political issues than any other source. Racism ranks high as a complaint but not sexism in most sources. The "occult," "secular humanism", and new right organizations can be found in all but Woods' research, however, the occult appears to be a significant concern in the most recent decade, while secular humanism complaints are less predominant in the data (Table 5.9).

THE OUTCOMES OF CENSORSHIP: PAST AND PRESENT

The results of the censorship attempts were tracked as much as possible for the current four sources, and were categorized by type of result. This categorization was compiled from the information provided by Burress in his table of

Table 5.10 Results of Censorship Attempts

RESULT/ SOURCE	NIF	SPLC	CN	ATFL	BU
REVIEW COMMITTEE					
kept	100				
restricted use	21		1		
required parental permission	13			11	
moved item to higher level	5				1
banned, canceled	30			2	
SCHOOL/ LIBRARY BOARD					
kept	288	24	2		3
restricted use	26		5	13	
required parental permission	24		1		
banned, canceled	87			9	2
READING LISTS					
kept on required	8				
kept on optional	6		2		
moved from required to optional	13			6	4
kept with alternative available	12			4	
OTHER RESULTS: SUCCESSFUL ATTEMPTS					
banned	393	42	21	78	424
canceled	115	2		18	10
cut, pasted, glued over	69	11	3	4	24
rejected for inclusion	50	5	5	2	
ban upheld in court	37	14			7
editor, staff suspended or fired	33	37	1	2	5
people involved threatened with arrest or arrested	33				
destroyed/ vandalized	30	3	1		14
student suspended or expelled	28	17			
editor, staff, advisor resigned	14	3		1	1
item stolen, checked out and not returned,	12	8		1	4
police, authority seized or canceled	10				
librarian, author, etc. threatened or harmed	6	1			
copies seized		20			
blank page or "censored" printed		2			
newspaper closed permanently		1			
apology or retraction					5
OTHER ACTION: UNSUCCESSFUL					
item kept	75		8	4	341
court struck down ban	62	28	3		12
complaint withdrawn	2	1			
library added item to collection	1				1

Table 5.10 (continued)

RESULT/SOURCE	NIF	SPLC	CN	ATFL	BU
OTHER ACTION: PARTIALLY SUCCESSFUL					
item moved to higher level	31		1	16	5
new guidelines for selection, removal	30	20	1		3
item delayed from release	25	9			
funding reduced or eliminated	18	12		2	
legislature introduced or passed legislation against such items	10				
substituted or abridged	8		1	14	
program changed time, location, station	3				
newspaper closed temporarily		5			
restricted to campus distribution		4			
restricted shelf					144
alternative selection provided					123
removed temporarily					24
required parental permission					2
OTHER ACTION: STILL PENDING, OTHER					
no action taken or mentioned	15		1		36
complaint filed, no action taken	289	33	8		
boycotted, protested	84	7			
citizen, student author defended item	36				
decision postponed	12				
testimony against item	10				
parties settled out of court	7				
still being reviewed					16
other					10

Sources: Newsletter on Intellectual Freedom (1981-1990); *Student Press Law Center Report* (1981-1990); *Censorship News* (1981-1990); *Attacks on the Freedom to Learn* (1982-1990); Burress (1989).

survey data, as well (see Table 5.10). However, Woods has not categorized the outcomes of censorship attempts he discovered in the 1966-1975 *NIF* issues with as much specification as is possible in the other sources. Instead, he groups the statistics into the number of "successful" and "unsuccessful" censorship attempts, with two other categories for "partially successful" attempts and "result not given." To make these comparisons, the more specific outcomes of Burress' data and of this research have been classified into the four Woods' groupings (see Table 5.11). A successful attempt is one that has resulted in removing or denying access to the created work. This includes banning, removing, or canceling the item in question, or destroying, stealing, or editing or cutting out the offensive content. Where incidents occurred in which the librarian, teacher, editor, creator, or other person attempting to protect the work has been harmed in some way, included being fired, expelled, or suspended, a "successful" attempt has been recorded because the work was also shown to be removed in these cases. An unsuccessful attempt is one that resulted in the work remaining available at the level for which it was intended. For instance, if a book was part of an optional reading list and was kept on that list after the complaint was filed, it has been considered an unsuccessful attempt. A partially successful attempt category has been used to group attempts for which the outcome has not denied access but places some type of restriction that limits access, such as requirements for parental permission or having the work in a restricted area, or at a higher age level. In instances where a required reading was made optional, this has been considered a partially successful attempt. The fourth category is used to group challenges that have no determination. Such incidents are most often from reports early in the challenge where a complaint has been filed but no action has been taken or recorded.

A comparison of the rates of successful, unsuccessful and partially successful censorship attempts in all six sources indicates that a successful attempt has occurred more often than any other result (see Table 5.11). The reports of successful attempts range from a low of 40.38% in Burress' thirty-five-year study to a high of 62.23% in the *ATFL* for 1981-1990. This is an average of 49.52% or almost half of all attempts result in a successful act of censorship. However, an examination of all the data shows that the percentages for all the sources except the *Attacks on the Freedom to Learn* do not vary substantially from each other in the four types of results. The *ATFL*, however, reports only 2.13% unsuccessful attempts, well below the 21.81% reported by the *SPLC*

Table 5.11 Results of Censorship Challenges Ranked According to Percentage Success

RESULT/ SOURCE	NIF (%)	SPLC (%)	CN (%)	ATFL (%)	BU(%)	WOODS (%)
successful	43.56	52.53	48.44	64.36	40.38	51.3
unsuccessful	24.93	16.77	23.44	2.13	29.36	28.0
partially successful	10.99	17.72	14.06	33.51	25.16	7.8
other	20.52	12.98	14.06	0.00	5.1	12.9

Sources: Newsletter on Intellectual Freedom (1981-1990); Student Press Law Center Report (1981-1990); Censorship News (1981-1990); Attacks on the Freedom to Learn (1982-1990); Burress (1989).

Report, the next lowest percentage for this category. If the *ATFL* data is filtered out, the other five sources average 46.98% successful censorship attempts, and their range varies only from a low of 40.38% reported by Burress to a high of 53.27% reported by the *SPLC Report* for 1981-1990 (see Table 5.11).

The percentage of unsuccessful censorship attempts also is relatively constant across the sources, except for the *Attacks on the Freedom to Learn* as well (Table 5.11). This data shows that an average of 25.54% of all censorship attempts are unsuccessful, as reported by the remaining five sources, ranging from a low of 16.51% of the *SPLC Report* to a high of 29.36% of the Burress study. These sets of data appear to show that, on the average, about twice as many attempts to censor will be successful as unsuccessful, with approximately another 15% of all attempts resulting in a partial censorship action.

FOUR CENSORSHIP PERIODICALS COMPARED

This chapter has made a comparison of the statistics gathered from the sources of the 1980s with the two historical studies, but a general comparison of the value of the four periodicals studied as chronicles of censorship information is also necessary to gauge the usefulness of each of these titles for censorship research. Such a comparison will aid in evaluating the findings reported in this study and for determining the value of these sources for future research.

Each of these four periodicals is published by a nationally prominent, intellectual freedom organization whose primary purpose is to combat censorship. However, most of their other attributes beyond this fact are very different. The *Newsletter on Intellectual Freedom* published by the American Library Association's Office for Intellectual Freedom, has a primary audience among librarians and libraries. The *Attacks on the Freedom to Learn*, published by the People for the American Way (PAW), is an annual report for the membership of the PAW, which consists mainly of civil libertarians and liberal activists. The National Coalition Against Censorship, publisher of *Censorship News*, consists of library and book trade organizations and many other professional associations concerned about censorship; therefore, it has a somewhat similar audience to that of the first two newsletters, but focused on censorship entirely. The *Student Press Law Center Report* is a specialized journal and its audience is narrowly focused toward the student press.

In addition to a different audience, the types of censorship reported differ in at least three of the four sources. The *Student Press Law Center Report* only records censorship attempts of student publications in secondary schools and colleges, although it includes publications other than student newspapers. *Censorship News* and the *Attacks on the Freedom to Learn* limit their coverage to schools and academic institutions. However, the *Newsletter on Intellectual Freedom* does not limit what type of censorship challenge is included in each issue. It reports incidents in such institutions as retail stores, museums, concert halls, the publishing industry, prisons, and public forums, as well as schools, colleges, and libraries.

There is also a distinctive variation in the number of reports in each title and the richness of data in the reports. Table 5.12 shows the number of issues per year, the average number of incidents reported in each issue and the total number of incidents for this ten year period of research for each of the four sources. This table demonstrates that there is a far greater average number of incidents reported each year by the *Newsletter on Intellectual Freedom* than any of the other three sources, and a far larger total for this decade than the other three titles. The *NIF* published 52.9 times more reports than *Censorship News*, nine times more than the *Student Press Law Center Report*, and 6.5 times more than the *Attacks on the Freedom to Learn*. Furthermore, the *Newsletter* often contains follow-ups to earlier censorship incidents, tracking many of them from the original attempt or complaint to the final result, on many occasions as far as federal court action. Many of the reports in the *NIF, Censorship News,* and the

Table 5.12 Comparison of Numbers of Issues and Reports in Four Censorship Sources

CHARACTERISTICS/ SOURCE	NIF	CN	ATFL	SPLC
Number of Issues Per Year	6	4	1	3
Average Number of Censorship Reports Per Issue	35.26	1	38.2	7.8
Average Number of Censorship Reports Per Year	211.6	4	38.2	23.4
Total Number of Censorship Reports (1981-1990)	2116	40	344	234

Sources: Newsletter on Intellectual Freedom (1981-1990); Censorship News (1981-1990); Attacks on the Freedom to Learn (1982-1990); Student Press Law Center Report (1981-1990).

Student Press Law Center Report contain most of the first nine categories of data, often with considerable detail, but the early issues of the *Attacks on the Freedom to Learn* tend to be sketchy. Although the *SPLC Report* publishes far fewer reports of censorship, almost 90% of their reports concern challenges to the student press. The *NIF* includes 151 challenges to the student press in the 1980s compared to at least 217 compiled in the *Student Press Law Center Report*.

The format or layout of each issue and of the articles included in them are different as well. The *Newsletter on Intellectual Freedom* and the *SPLC Report* use topical sub-sections that address censorship issues germane to the audiences they address. Both titles provide a report on current judicial activity of relevance as well. The *Attacks on the Freedom to Learn* presents a review of the year's events as an annual report, then lists incidents by state in what is called "The 50 State Report." *Censorship News* utilizes a newspaper or newsletter format of articles, sometimes with a theme to the issue. The entries in *Censorship News* and the *SPLC Report* contain reports that are usually page length or more, whereas the *NIF* is one to two paragraphs, one newsprint column wide. The *NIF* often includes valuable quotes from the complainant as well as the advocates. The *ATFL* has the best layout for this type of research. Each major attribute is labeled separately, including "Incident," which tells the basic facts of the case, "Initiator" (or complainant), and "Resolution," which provides information on the results of the attempt.

This research shows that the *Newsletter on Intellectual Freedom*, published by the American Library Association, is the best source for data on censorship. It reports far more incidents than any other source, and the types of incidents run the full spectrum of challenges. Despite the relatively small size of each report, as compared with those of *Censorship News* and the *SPLC Report*, each report has a richness of data that more than meets the needs of this type of research.

The *Student Press Law Center Report* is an excellent compliment to the *Newsletter*. Although it reports far fewer challenges, its specialized focus makes it superior to the *NIF* in reporting threats to the student press. Not only does it report more incidents of student press censorship, but also its coverage of each incident is more in depth than the news items of the *Newsletter on Intellectual Freedom*. Furthermore, the coverage in the *SPLC Report* is unique compared with the individual titles reported in the *NIF*. Of 215 distinct titles in the *SPLC Report* issues, only sixty-seven were also reported in the *Newsletter* for the same time period.

The *Attacks on the Freedom to Learn* and *Censorship News* serve a useful purpose. Although they may lack a significantly weighty set of censorship data for this type of research, these publications are intended to act as a vehicle to combat censorship by providing their readers with a sample of the problem and energized discussions on the threat such actions pose. The censorship reports included in these publications serve this purpose in many ways and are often backed by inspiring essays. These two periodicals are worth consideration for collections on intellectual freedom and censorship.

6 Conclusion

HISTORICAL OVERVIEW

The decade 1981-1990 has now passed into the history books. On a national and international scale, there were many triumphs and many tragedies, some brought about by decisions of government and the people, in general, others as a natural consequence. This decade in the United States witnessed a new political era. What had been seen as a growth of liberalism in the 1960s and early 1970s as the Baby Boomer generation came of age during an unpopular war, had been reversed by a populace disillusioned with government because of Watergate in the early 1970s and because of governments inability to ameliorate severe economic conditions such as high inflation, a gasoline crisis, and rising unemployment in the late 1970s. In the presidential election of 1980, the people turned to former California Governor Ronald Reagan, who promised a return to family values on a political and social level, and economic prosperity by introducing supply-side economics. His political agenda on all fronts, international, domestic economy, and social policy, was decidedly conservative. He was elected with the help of conservative and fundamentalist Christian organizations whose agendas were openly announced as intending to reverse liberal gains in personal and social freedoms especially in abortion, civil liberties for the accused, and public education. There was no doubt in the minds of most liberals, including intellectual freedom advocates, that this meant a gloomy period for civil rights and civil liberties. In 1981, for example, it was reported that the American Civil Liberties Union experienced a tremendous surge in donations and new members. At the time it was thought that Reagan's conservative victory had shocked the liberal faithful out of their complacency.

There were other signals of this time to indicate that intellectual freedom may have fallen by the political wayside. Such incidents as the Abingdon, Virginia, Public Library case where popular pot-boiler novels were attacked by the Moral Majority served notice that censorship was indeed on the rise. More disturbing was the inevitable stacking of the Supreme Court with justices who would march lockstep to the conservative agenda, beginning with Reagan's elevation of William Rehnquist from associate to chief justice.

ANOTHER DECADE OF CENSORSHIP

It is with these events in mind that this research has begun with the belief that the 1980s would be a decade of massive censorship attacks, directed at not just hardcore pornography but all forms of expression. Previous studies, most notably L.B. Woods' *A Decade of Censorship in America* and Lee Burress' *The Battle of the Books*, have provided measurements of censorship, both by identifying a significant body of information on what has been censored and by compiling statistics on the level of censorship. These two research projects have demonstrated the fact that censorship in America is not primarily aimed at hardcore pornography, or for that matter, softcore pornography, but most often against school and library books, particularly young adult and classic literature. They have also indicated a general rise in censorship attempts, especially Woods' 1966-1975 research.

These two events--the rise of conservatism in 1980 and the growth of censorship in the 1970s--could only lead to the theory that this decade would experience high levels of censorship that would rise steadily throughout at least the tenure of Ronald Reagan. As mentioned earlier, if a "liberal" decade (1966-1975) could produce a "decade of censorship in America" (Woods 1979), a conservative decade should produce at least as much, if not more, censorship challenges.

This research was designed to replicate the general research goals of L. B. Woods' *A Decade of Censorship in America* (1979). This work has not duplicated his research, but instead has attempted to, first, extend the value of his study by performing a similar statistical survey on a more current set of data, and second, to improve his research design by expanding the research questions asked and by increasing the sources of censorship data. It is this kind of research design that is the heart of any statistical analysis of censorship. By asking the set of research questions that have been posed and by compiling data from at least one source of censorship incidents, basic and valuable conclusions can be reached concerning the level, type, and effect of censorship for a given time period.

This project has found that the theory of a conservative tide toward a greater level of censorship held true for only the first part of the 1980s. This was most certainly realized in 1981, the first year of Reagan's triumph. At least 365 cases of censorship were recorded by one of the reporting sources. This was not as significant as the final year of Woods' study (1975), which realized 563 incidents from the same source. No other year in the 1980s decade reached this level of censorship. The remaining Reagan years averaged 252 reports in the *Newsletter on Intellectual Freedom*. Furthermore, the *NIF* reported almost exactly the same number of challenges from 1981-1990 as it did from 1966-1975: 2,174 in the current decade and 2,178 in the earlier research.

By the 1988 election year, which saw the ascension of George Bush, Reagan's vice-president, to the presidency, the decline in the number of reported censorship cases began. By the final year of this decade, the level of censorship reached a low of fifty-one, equivalent to the earliest years of Woods' research. The face of conservatism had changed, although it was still very much active, but the growth of censorship had not been evident in the reporting sources. Such a phenomena may not be surprising. Reagan was not known for his support of libraries, for example, but President Bush and his wife, especially, have been strong supporters of libraries and literacy programs.

THE JUDY BLUME DECADE

As in past research, censorship occurs against well-known literary works and children's or young adult literature. Both L. B. Woods (1979) and Lee Burress (1989) found *Catcher in the Rye* by J. D. Salinger to be the most censored material, Woods for just 1966-1975 and Burress over thirty-five-years of survey data. The face of censorship has changed, however, in the 1980s. *Playboy* magazine is the most censored item in the United States. Although periodical censorship was also much greater in the 1980s than in the past, books are still the most challenged format and Judy Blume's *Deenie*, not *Catcher in the Rye*, is the most censored book.

More importantly, it can be said that this has been the decade of the attack on Judy Blume. Not only is *Deenie* the most censored book of the 1980s, but also five of the ten most challenged books are written by Blume, including the three most censored books discovered in this research. No other author in this study or in any other research examined has been subject to as much vilification or objections as Judy Blume has during the 1980s. There were a few incidents reported that challenged all of her works, not just a specific title, indicating that these challenges go beyond content objections to attacks on the author herself.

To be sure, there have been significant challenges to numerous works other than those written by Judy Blume. It has been demonstrated that only Salinger's *Catcher in the Rye* and *Go Ask Alice*, written anonymously, have been the target of the censor more often during all of the decades covered by this and the two other studies (Woods 1979; Burress 1989) than any other book. Furthermore, the 1980s witnessed continued attacks on several American classics, including *The Adventures of Huckleberry Finn* by Mark Twain and *Of Mice and Men* and *The Grapes of Wrath* by John Steinbeck.

FIVE CONSISTENT ATTRIBUTES OF A CENSORSHIP CHALLENGE

Many of the attributes of a censorship challenge have not changed over time, at least as to what has been regarded as the most significant individual contributor to each attribute. This research design has asked several questions to discover where the variations lie in each category of the anatomy of a censorship attempt. Five of these queries found that no major difference exists in what has been recorded as the primary characteristic of these attributes over time. This and all other sources have found that the book is by far the most challenged format. What has been discovered, however, is that periodical censorship has surpassed all other formats as the next most troublesome type of expressive work. Both Woods and Burress report less than 3% of all materials in their research were magazines,but this study recorded almost 10% of all incidents to have been periodical censorship.

Additionally, this and Woods' (1979) studies found that high schools experience more censorship attempts than any other institution. Despite the focus on educational institutions of Woods' and Burress' research, however, the current research has found more systemic censorship against most educational institutions. During the 1980s, the *Newsletter on Intellectual Freedom* found all but junior high schools and junior high libraries to each have accounted for almost 10% of all censorship incidents, or more. Woods reported only high schools, public libraries, and colleges to constitute 10% or more of the data.

Throughout the years and across all sources of book censorship, "parents" have consistently been the most likely category of complainants to object to the content of an expressive work. Although there are a number of variations in the relative rankings of the remaining categories of complainants, this research has also found that the current book censorship sources show that most censors are individuals with a specific local interest in the institution where the attack is occurring. More often, the censor is someone who is either employed by the institution, attends it as a student, or is a member of the governing board. Furthermore, three other types of local individuals also produce almost as much, if not more, censorship complaints as those persons directly affiliated with the institution: (1) parents whose children attend the institution, (2) ministers who are considered to be members of the community's extended family, and (3) citizens who pay taxes to the institutions and who may have children or grandchildren in attendance at the school.

A substantial number of outside pressure groups has not been found in the data, although some influence is evident. Censorship by nationally affiliated groups has accounted for 8% of all attempts reported in the *Newsletter*. Furthermore, the political orientation of the national interest groups found in these reports is decidedly conservative. Of the twenty-three known organizations mentioned as a complainant during the 1980s in the *Newsletter on Intellectual Freedom*, sixteen are known to serve a conservative agenda, whereas only four are considered liberal. In 1966-1975, the John Birch Society and the PTA were the most predominant censors. During the 1980s, no source reported a censorship attempt by the John Birch Society. Instead Phyllis Schafly's Eagle Forum has been mentioned the most as a complainant in a censorship controversy.

One exception to the pattern of "parent" as the most frequent complainant has been noted in the *Student Press Law Center Report*. The statistics for the 1980s in this publication show that the "principal" and other institutional authorities as the primary source of censorship complaints against the student press. Parental objections play a very minor role in the censorship of student publications. Authority and control, rather than objectionable content, are the reasons seen for institutional demands on student journalism.

A fourth attribute, the reason for the objection, remains constant as well. This research corroborates past findings that sexually related content, in several forms, is by far the most frequent objection to books and other forms of expression. The data from the *Newsletter on Intellectual Freedom* for 1981-1990 has been grouped into sixty-three categories, only eight of which have a sexual theme. However, these eight categories account for 50.7% of all complaints. All other sources examined for this research report similar data. When an objection is made against an item, it has most often been because of "profanity," "obscenity," or general sexual themes. It had been theorized that some nonsexual themes, especially those that are offensive to new right organizations, particularly the "occult," "evolution," and "anti-family values," would play a very dominant role in these findings. Only charges that a work has been "anti-Christian" have received as much predominance in the data, and to some degree, "occult" complaints.

Last, the most common result of a censorship complaint appears to be the same as reported by L. B. Woods. He analyzed the final outcome of each incident in the decade of 1966-1975 and found that more attempts concluded with a decision to censor the work than to protect it or a partial solution that limited access without censoring altogether. Although the proportions of such outcomes are slightly different in each source, the current research also demonstrates that the outcome of a censorship attempt is most likely to be a successful challenge to a form of expression. More cases have been recorded wherein the item has been banned than any other single result.

This research, however, has discovered a difference in the decision made by governing boards from that of individual authorities. Although all manner of authoritative decisions have concluded with a ban on some materials, individual authorities, such as principals, directors, librarians, teachers, and business managers or owners, have banned expression more often than governing boards. A school board, library board or appointed review committee is more likely to reject a challenge than ban an item. However, the data for 1981-1990 indicates that individuals in authority have ruled in favor of the complaint in at least three fourths of all such cases.

A NEW ATTRIBUTE TO RESEARCH: THE ADVOCATES

Most censorship research has generally attempted to identify the causes and contributing factors of content objections. The focus of such research is naturally on who the complainants are because they are seen as either a cause or a contributing factor to an act of censorship. However, information gathered only on those who complain about a form of expression tells only half the story of the case.   When a censorship incident occurs, there are usually two viewpoints, pro and con, and there are often two corresponding forces, defenders and objectors, that can influence the outcome. Although it is important to measure the efforts of the complainants, it is also important to identify the advocates and gauge the impact they have on censorship activity.   This information can aid in a fuller understanding of what constitutes successful and unsuccessful complaints.

This research has found that teachers, including college professors and teacher associations, are the most frequent advocate. The design of this study has excluded most teachers who have defended challenged materials used in their own classroom or who have been the target of the censor themselves, therefore, this represents, primarily, teachers who have not been directly affected by the challenge. Because of the definition of an advocate for this study excluded librarians and teachers directly effected by the complaint, such individuals who would normally be considered advocates have been arbitrarily excluded, though, more data is needed to make such conclusions. Furthermore, it has been discovered that the American Civil Liberites Union is the most frequent nationally affiliated organization to provide a defense for a challenged form of expression. These results, however, have been gleaned from a relatively small data set collected from the *Newsletter on Intellectual Freedom*. An advocate has not ususally been mentioned in most censorship accounts. There may be a need for reporting sources to include such information in future reports.

SUMMARY OF CONCLUSIONS

This research began by asking ten questions. It has found that the 1980s decade had approximately the same level of censorship as that reported by L. B. Woods (1979) for the decade 1966-1975, that is, 2,174 incidents of censorship, which addresses the first question about the total amount of censorship. It also found that the most censored material is *Playboy* magazine and the most censored book is Judy Blume's *Deenie,* which attends to Questions 1 and 2 on the total amount and the targets of censorship. The remaining answers to the questions posed for the 1980s are as follows.

Question 3: Censored formats--Books remain the most challenged form of expresssion. However, periodical censorship has risen over that reported by Woods (1979) and Burress (1989).

Question 4: Years of Censorship--the first year of the decade, 1981, experienced the most challenges. Most of the Reagan years witnessed substatial numbers of censorship incidents. The number of reported cases began to decline in 1988 and through the first years of George Bush's presidency, according to *NIF.*

Question 5: States Where Censorship Occurred the Most--During the 1980s, the concentration of censorship, as calculated by indexing the number of attempts reported to the population of the states, was the greatest in the farm-belt Midwestern states and the Western states, especially the Pacific Northwest.

Question 6: Censored Institutions--Educational institutions remain the target of the censor especially high schools and high school libraries. However, retail outlets such as bookstores and department stores, have been the non-educational institution attacked most often.

Question 7: The Complainants--Parents, as a category, have remained the most frequent complainant in censorship cases. It has also been shown that most objections originate with an individual who has a direct link to an educational institution, such as a student, principal, or school board member, or a vested interest in the school, such as a parent, minister, or local resident or citizen.

Question 8: The Objections--Sexual content, in various forms, has caused the most difficulties for all forms of expression. This is another conclusion that has not changed from that of past research.

Question 9: The Outcomes of Censorship Attempts--As has been reported by L. B. Woods (1979) and Lee Burress (1989), a censorship challenge is more likely to succeed in banning or otherwise limiting an expressive work than to fail to ban or restrict access to its use.

Question 10: The Advocates--Teachers, especially those not directly effected by the censorship challenge, are the most frequent advocates of a banned book or other expressive form. Furthermore, the American Civil Liberties Union is the most active national organization in the direct defense of challenged materials.

The 1980s were another decade of censorship. At least as many challenges happened from 1980 to 1990 as in any other ten-year period measured in the past. The most striking facet of this era is undoubtedly the strength of attacks on the works of Judy Blume, a young adult novelist. With as many charges of objectionable material from every corner of the censorious population, the 1980s can truly be labeled "The Decade of the Attack on Judy Blume."

Appendix: Challenged Titles Listed in All Four Sources in Order of Frequency of Challenge

TITLE	NUMBER OF CHALLENGES	AUTHOR (BOOKS) OR FORMAT
NEWSLETTER ON INTELLECTUAL FREEDOM		
Playboy	47	magazine
Penthouse	25	magazine
Deenie	18	Blume
Forever	17	Blume
Then Again, Maybe I Won't	17	Blume
The Adventures of Huckleberry Finn	16	Twain
Of Mice and Men	15	Steinbeck
Show Me!	15	McBride
Go Ask Alice	13	Anonymous
Blubber	11	Blume
Catcher in the Rye	11	Salinger
Are You There, God? It's Me, Margaret	10	Blume
Doonesbury	10	comic
Dungeons & Dragons	10	game
Hustler	10	magazine
Playgirl	10	magazine
The Last Temptation of Christ	9	film
Changing Bodies, Changing Lives	9	Bell
The Chocolate War	9	Cormier
Our Bodies, Ourselves	9	Boston Women's Health
The Color Purple	8	Walker
A Light in the Attic	8	Silverstein
Slaughterhouse Five	8	Vonnegut
Sports Illustrated Swimsuit Issue	7	magazine
The Crucible	6	Miller
Flowers for Algernon	6	Keyes
Married and Single Life	6	textbook
Oui	6	magazine
Sister Mary Ignatius Explains It All for You	6	play
To Kill a Mockingbird	6	Lee

TITLE	NUMBER OF CHALLENGES	AUTHOR (BOOKS) OR FORMAT
Brave New World	5	Huxley
Cujo	5	King
A Day No Pigs Would Die	5	Peck
Deep Throat	5	film
Finding My Way	5	textbook
Hail Mary	5	film
Impressions	5	textbook
Ms.	5	magazine
Romeo and Juliet	5	film
Vsion Quest	5	Davis
Where the Sidewalk Ends	5	Silverstein
Biology	4	textbook
Bloodline	4	Sheldon
Chic	4	magazine
Debbie Does Dallas	4	film
Grapes of Wrath	4	Steinbeck
High Society	4	magazine
I Know Why the Caged Birds Sings	4	Angelou
Issues and Answers	4	magazine
It's Not the End of the World	4	Blume
It's OK if You Don't Love Me	4	Klein
Let's Talk About Health	4	textbook
Lord of the Flies	4	Golding
Modern Human Sexuality	4	textbook
Oh! Calcutta!	4	play
Ordinary People	4	Guest
Playboy Channel	4	television
Rolling Stone	4	magazine
Run, Shelley, Run!	4	Samuels
Salem's Lot	4	King
The Shining	4	King
Where Do Babies Come from?	4	Mahle
Adolescents Today	3	textbook
Birth of a Nation	3	film
Boys and Sex	3	Pomeroy
Christine	3	King
Dartmouth Review	3	student newspaper
Death of a Salesman	3	Miller
Dondi	3	comic
Family Matters	3	textbook
Firestarter	3	King
The Great Gatsby	3	Fitzgerald
The Great Gilly Hopkins	3	Peterson
Grendel	3	Gardner
Hard Feelings	3	Fell
Headman	3	Platt
Humanities: Cultural Roots & Continuities	3	textbook

TITLE	NUMBER OF CHALLENGES	AUTHOR (BOOKS) OR FORMAT
In the Spirit of Crazy Horse	3	Matthiessen
Joy of Sex	3	Comfort
La Cage Aux Folles	3	film
Last Mission	3	Mazer
Last Tango in Paris	3	film
Caligula	3	film
Life	3	magazine
Manchild in the Promised Land	3	Brown
Married Life	3	textbook
National Lampoon	3	magazine
Newsweek	3	magazine
Once is Not Enough	3	Susann
One Flew Over the Cuckoo's Nest	3	Kesey
Our Land, Our Time	3	Conlin
Ozzy Osbourne concert	3	music
Penthouse Forum	3	magazine
Person to Person	3	textbook
Petals on the Wind	3	Andrews
photographs	3	art
Pippin	3	play
A Separate Peace	3	Knowles
The Sisters Impossible	3	Landis
Sociology	3	textbook
South End	3	student newspaper
Spermbusters	3	film
Starring Sally J. Freedman as Herself	3	Blume
Story of O	3	film
Street Law	3	textbook
Tiger Eyes	3	Blume
TV 101	3	television
Understanding Health	3	textbook
Understanding Your Sexuality	3	textbook
Valley of the Horses	3	Auel
Witches	3	Dahl
Working	3	Terkel
About Sex	2	film
Achieving Sexual Maturity	2	film
Adventurers	2	Robbins
Albert Hawkins and the Space Rocket	2	Dickens
Albert Hawkins, the Naughtiest Boy in the World	2	Dickens
all adult magazines	2	magazine
Ancient Evenings	2	Mailer
Angel Dust Blues	2	Strasser
Animal Farm	2	Orwell
Annie on My Mind	2	Garden
Batman and Daffy Duck comics	2	comic

TITLE	NUMBER OF CHALLENGES	AUTHOR (BOOKS) OR FORMAT
Before You Were a Baby	2	Showers
Best Little Whorehouse in Texas	2	play
Bloods: An Oral History of the Vietnam War by Black Veterans	2	Terry
books on witchcraft	2	book
Boss	2	Royko
bumper stickers	2	other
Call of the Wild	2	film/ book (London)
Carrie	2	film/ book (King)
Children of the Corn	2	film/ book (King)
Children's Hour	2	play
Chisholms	2	Hunter
Confessions of an Only Child	2	Klein
Cosmopolitan	2	magazine
Curses, Hexes, and Spells	2	Cohen
Diary of Anne Frank	2	Goodrich
Different Seasons	2	King
Doctor Love	2	Greene
Dressed to Kill	2	film
Equus	2	play
Facts About Sex, a Basic Guide	2	Gordon
Facts of Love	2	Comfort
Fahrenheit 451	2	Bradbury
Fields of Fire	2	Webb
Fort Apache, the Bronx	2	film
gay pride exhibit	2	exhibit
Gentlehands	2	Kerr
Golden Book of the Mysterious	2	Watson
Gone With the Wind	2	Mitchell
Grease	2	play
Great Cities	2	Time-Life
Ground Zero	2	newspaper
Hamlet	2	textbook (Shakespeare)
Happy Endings are All Alike	2	Scoppetone
Haunted by the Holy Ghost	2	play
Health	2	textbook
Health (by John LaPlace)	2	textbook
Hearts and Minds	2	film
Hoof Beat	2	student newspaper
Hortensia Allende (widow of Salvador Allende of Chile)	2	speech
How Babies are Made	2	Hodges
Humanist	2	magazine
I Am the Cheese	2	Cormier
I Love You, Stupid	2	Mazer
I Want Your Sex (by George Michael)	2	music
I'm Mad at You	2	Cole
Image of the Beast	2	Farmer

TITLE	NUMBER OF CHALLENGES	AUTHOR (BOOKS) OR FORMAT
In Cold Blood	2	play/ book (Capote)
In the Night Kitchen	2	Sendak
Inherit the Wind	2	play/ film
Inheritors	2	Robbins
Inserts	2	film
Inside Mom	2	Caveney
Introduction to Myth	2	textbook
Julie of the Wolves	2	George
Killing of Mr. Griffin	2	Duncan
Life and Health	2	textbook
Literature of the Supernatural	2	Beck
Lonely Lady	2	Robbins
Lottery	2	film
Love and Sex in Plain Language	2	Johnson
Lysistrata	2	textbook
Mademoiselle	2	magazine
Martian Chronicles	2	Bradbury
Matematicheski Sbornik	2	magazine
Men in Love	2	Friday
Merriam-Webster New Collegiate Dictionary	2	Merriam-Webster
Miller's Tale	2	textbook
Minnesota Daily	2	student newspaper
Mister Roberts	2	play/ book (Heggen)
Monsters	2	book
Mother Goose (Viking Press edition)	2	book
My Darling, My Hamburger	2	Zindel
My Sweet Audrina	2	Andrews
National Geographic	2	magazine
Never Cry Wolf	2	film/ book (Mowat)
Night Shift	2	King
nude dancers	2	other
Oedipus Rex	2	Sophocles
Omaha, the Cat Dancer	2	comic
Outsiders	2	Hinton
Penthouse advertisements	2	advertisements
People	2	magazine
People Like Us	2	television
photography exhibit	2	exhibit
Pink Floyd- The Wall	2	film
political advertisements	2	advertisements
posters	2	other
Principles of Science I and II	2	textbook
Pumsey Program	2	other/ book
Quartzite Trip	2	Hogan
Rambler	2	student newspaper
Recreational Drugs	2	book
Revolutionary Worker	2	newspaper

TITLE	NUMBER OF CHALLENGES	AUTHOR (BOOKS) OR FORMAT
Ride the Silver Seas	2	textbook/ book
Robert M. Burger (impressionist)	2	speech
rock and roll music	2	music
San Quentin News	2	newspaper
school mascot (Red Devil)	2	other
school yearbook	2	student press
sculpture	2	art
Seven Arrows	2	Stonm
Shane	2	Schaefer
Single and Pregnant	2	Pierce
Slugs	2	Hutson
Soledad Star News	2	newspaper
Spectrum	2	student newspaper
street preacher	2	speech
student variety show	2	play
Stupids Die	2	Allard
Superfudge	2	Blume
Taxi Zum Klo	2	film
That Was Then, This is Now	2	Hinton
three photographs	2	art
Tin Drum	2	film
Topics for the Restless	2	Spargo
Understanding Psychology	2	textbook
Velvet	2	magazine
Warriors	2	film
A Way of Love, A Way of Life	2	Hankel
Weirdo	2	comic
What is a Boy? What is a Girl?	2	Waxman
When the Sky Began to Roar	2	Bach
Winning	2	Brancato
Witchcraft, Mysticism, and Magic in the Black World	2	Haskins
Witches, Witches, Witches	2	book
You and Your Health	2	textbook
Young and Black in America	2	Alexander
17 books	1	book
1982 Cat Hater's Calendar	1	other
8 books on human sexuality at 8 elementary schools	1	textbook
Abdul Hassan (PLO UN Representative)	1	speech
Abortion and the Conscience of the Nation	1	Reagan
About David	1	Pfaffer
About Last Night	1	film
Absolutes	1	magazine
Abu Zanib (Iraqi excile)	1	speech
Accommodation: The Politics of Race in an American City	1	Schutze
Acid From Heaven	1	film

TITLE	NUMBER OF CHALLENGES	AUTHOR (BOOKS) OR FORMAT
Acid Rain: Requiem or Recovery?	1	film
Act of Marriage	1	La Haye
Actor's Book of Contemporary Stage Monologues	1	book
Acts of Violence	1	television
Adam's Daughter	1	Bloom
Adolfo Colero	1	speech
adult book store	1	other
adult magazines	1	magazine
Adventures in English Literature	1	textbook
advertisement for Miller Brewing Co.	1	advertisement
advertisements for American-Arab Committee	1	advertisement
advertisements for an art exhibit	1	advertisement
advertisements for gay housing	1	advertisement
advertisements for Jews for Jesus	1	advertisement
Advocate	1	magazine
Africans	1	television
After the First Death	1	Cormier
Against All Odds	1	Helms
AIDS Demographics	1	Crimp
Airplane	1	film
Al Exandra the Great	1	book
Alan and Naomi	1	Levey
Alan Dixon	1	speech
Alas, Babylon	1	Frank
Album	1	play
Album Cover Album	1	book
Alfred Hitchcock's Witches Brew	1	Hitchcock
Alfred Summer	1	Slepian
Alice With the Golden Hair	1	Hull
all Sol Gordon books	1	Gordon
Alone	1	Small
Amazine Bone	1	Steig
America Bewitched	1	Logan
America Reads	1	textbook
America, America	1	textbook
America: Focus on Literature	1	textbook
American Book English	1	textbook
American Dream	1	art
American English Today	1	textbook
American Foreign Policy, Volume II	1	textbook
American Heritage Dictionary	1	book
American Literature (Macmillan Edition)	1	textbook
American Pageant, Volume II	1	textbook
Americans All	1	textbook
Americans of Dream and Deed	1	textbook
Amiri Baraka	1	speech

TITLE	NUMBER OF CHALLENGES	AUTHOR (BOOKS) OR FORMAT
Amityville Horror	1	Ansan
Amy Girl	1	Wood
An Interview with God	1	play
Anastasia at Your Service	1	Lowry
Anastasia Krupnik	1	Lowry
And Miss Reardon Drinks a Little	1	play
And Still I Rise	1	Angelou
Angela Davis	1	speech
anonymously written newspaper articles	1	newspaper
anonymous political advertisements	1	advertisement
anti-nuclear drawing on sidewalk	1	art
anti-nuclear posters and button	1	other
anti-nuclear protestors	1	other
anti-Reagan political advertisement	1	advertisement
anti-smoking television advertisement	1	advertisement
Ape Men of Africa	1	film
Arab Radio Hour (KQED radio program)	1	radio
Arabs	1	textbook
arboretum exhibit	1	exhibit
archaeological exhibit	1	exhibit
archaeological exhibit from Israel	1	exhibit
archetypical feminine symbols	1	exhibit
Around the World with Jonny Wadd	1	film
Arrangement in Literature	1	textbook
Arts Focus	1	student press
As I Lay Dying	1	Faulkner
Astrology and Other Occult Games	1	Rowan
attorney's advertisements	1	advertisements
Autobiography of Benjamin Franklin	1	Franklin
Autumn Street	1	Lowry
Baby Starts to Grow	1	Showers
Babylon Motel	1	play
Bachman Books	1	King
Badge of the Assassin	1	television
Bag One	1	art
Ballad of Cable Hogue	1	film
Bang, Bang! You're Dead	1	Fisher
Bare-Faced Messiah: The True Story of L. Ron Hubbard	1	Miller
Battle of the Sexes	1	play
Bear Facts	1	student newspaper
Beat the Turtle Drum	1	Greene
Beauty of Birth	1	Portal
beer label	1	other
Beggar Man, Thief	1	book
Being There	1	Kosinski
Bell Jar	1	Plath

TITLE	NUMBER OF CHALLENGES	AUTHOR (BOOKS) OR FORMAT
Bent	1	play
Bernadette Devlin	1	speech
Best Short Stories	1	book
Bethany Hour	1	radio
Between Friends	1	Garrigue
Between Pride and Passion	1	Kidd
Beulah Land	1	television
BFG	1	Dahl
Bible	1	book
Bible class	1	other
Bible study classes	1	other
Biker's Lifestyle	1	magazine
Bill Grandall (retired U.S. Marine)	1	speech
billboard advertisements	1	advertisement
billboard art	1	art
billboards against Central American governments	1	advertisement
Biloxi Blues	1	play
Biographic Register	1	document
Biology, an Inquiry into the Nature of Life	1	textbook
Biology: An Everyday Experience	1	textbook
Bizarre Sex	1	comic
Black Boy	1	Wright
Black Focus	1	television
Black Magic, White Magic	1	Jennings
Black Marble	1	Randall
Black Poets	1	book
Bless the Beasts and the Children	1	Swarthout
Blood Brothers	1	book
Blood Feast	1	film
Bloom County	1	comic
Blue Lagoon	1	film
Blueboy	1	magazine
Bodyssey	1	comic
Boing!	1	newspaper
Bony-Legs	1	Cole
book display and exhibit	1	exhibit
Book of Lists	1	television
books by Norma Klein	1	Klein
books on witchcraft	1	book
books sponsored by Planned Parenthood	1	other
Booth	1	play
Boy and the Devil	1	Magnus
Boys at Bat	1	art
Brave New People	1	Jones
Breakfast Club	1	film
Brenda Dupris	1	speech
Brer Rabbit's Big Secret	1	play

TITLE	NUMBER OF CHALLENGES	AUTHOR (BOOKS) OR FORMAT
Bridge of Respect: Creating Support for Lesbian and Gay Youth	1	book
Bridge to Tarabithia	1	Paterson
Bridgewater Courier-News	1	newspaper
Bushwacker Times	1	student newspaper
Butterfly Revolution	1	Butler
Cabbage Patch Kids- The Just Right Family	1	book
Caleb- Issues and Answers	1	magazine
California Split	1	film
Came a Spider	1	Levy
Camel Tracks	1	student newspaper
Campanile	1	student newspaper
Campus News	1	student newspaper
campus radio program	1	radio
Cantebury Tales	1	Chaucer
Cardinal	1	student press
The Cardinal Detoxes	1	play
Caring, Deciding and Growing	1	textbook
Case of the Ancient Astronauts	1	Gallagher
Cat's Cradle	1	Vonnegut
Cathy	1	comic
Caught From Behind, Part II	1	film
CBS News	1	television
Chainsaw	1	music
Changes	1	Steele
Characters in Conflict	1	Warriner
Charger	1	student newspaper
Charlie Chan and the Curse of the Dragon Queen	1	film
Charlottesville Daily Progress	1	newspaper
Cheri	1	magazine
Chesty Morgan (striptease dancer)	1	dance
Chicago Mastery Reading Program	1	other
Child Growth and Development	1	textbook
Chimes	1	student newspaper
chocolate candies	1	other
Chocolate to Morphine	1	Weil
Choices: A Curriculum on Conflict and Nuclear War	1	other
Chopper Cycle	1	Radlauer
Chorus Line	1	play
Christmas Birthday Story	1	Laurence
Christmas carol program	1	music
Christmas Story	1	film
Chronicles of Narnia	1	Lewis
citizen of Hauppauge, NY	1	speech
city animal shelter flyer	1	other

TITLE	NUMBER OF CHALLENGES	AUTHOR (BOOKS) OR FORMAT
City Lights	1	television
City Times	1	student newspaper
Clarion	1	student newspaper
Clockwork Orange	1	Burgess
Clouds and Shadows	1	art
Colby Crossfire	1	student newspaper
Collected Poetry	1	book
College Daze	1	comic
College Heights Herald	1	student newspaper
College Voice	1	student newspaper
Color Me Blood Red	1	film
Comfort My People	1	radio
comic books	1	comic
comic books by Jack T. Chick	1	comic
commercial for Atheist group	1	adverstisement
Companion	1	magazine
Comparative Politics Today: A World View	1	textbook
Concepts in Biology	1	textbook
Confessions of Nat Turner	1	Styron
Contemporary Living	1	textbook
Contemporary Speech	1	textbook
The Cook, the Thief, His Wife and Her Lover	1	film
Coronado language series	1	textbook
Coser y Cantar	1	play
Cougar Growl	1	student newspaper
Cougar Times	1	student newspaper
Courier	1	student newspaper
course on homosexuality	1	other
Crazy	1	comic
Cream Circus	1	magazine
Creative Living	1	textbook
Crib	1	Friedman
Criterion	1	student newspaper
Crossings	1	Schneider
Crossroads	1	student newspaper
Crucifixion at Barton Creek Mall	1	art
Cue	1	other
Curse of the Starving Class	1	play
Custer's Revenge	1	game
Cycle of the Werewolf	1	King
Cystic Fibrosis Foundation advertisements	1	advertisement
Daily Banner	1	newspaper
Daily Fornicator	1	student newspaper
Daily Nebraskan	1	student newspaper
Daily Reveille	1	student newspaper
Daisy Canfeld	1	Haas

TITLE	NUMBER OF CHALLENGES	AUTHOR (BOOKS) OR FORMAT
Dakotas: At the Wind's Edge	1	Davis
Dale McCormick	1	speech
Dangerous Club	1	music
Daniel C. Maguire	1	speech
Dare to Discipline	1	Dobson
Dario Fo	1	speech
Dario Fo and Franca Rame (Italian political satirists)	1	speech
Dark of the Moon	1	play
Dartmouth Alumni Magazine	1	magazine
Daughters of the Sandino	1	art
David McCaldent's publishing display	1	exhibit
Days of Rage: The Young Palestinians	1	film
Dayton Daily News	1	newspaper
Dead Zone	1	King
Dear God by XTC	1	music
Death Be Not Proud	1	Gunther
Death of a Princess	1	television
Death of Arthur	1	book
Deathwatch	1	Trevor
debate between left-wing and right-wing group	1	speech
Deer Hunter	1	film
Delta Star	1	Wambaugh
Demons, Devils and Djinn	1	Hoyt
Desire Under the Elms	1	O'Neill
Devil in Miss Jones	1	film
Devil in the Drain	1	Pinkwater
Devil's Alternative	1	Forsyth
Devil's Book of Verse	1	Conniff
Devil's Music- A Blues Composition	1	music
Devil's Piper	1	Price
Devil's Storybook	1	Babbitt
Devils and Demons	1	Kaye
Diamondback	1	student newspaper
Diary of a Frantic Kid Sister	1	Coleman
Dictionary of American Slang	1	book
Dimensions in Life	1	textbook
Dinner Party	1	exhibit
display of homosexual books and artwork	1	exhibit
display on fortune telling	1	exhibit
display on homosexuality	1	exhibit
Doing Time	1	newspaper
Doctor Bey's Suicide Guidebook	1	Pell
Don and Donna Go To Bat	1	Perkins
Don't Tell Me Your Name	1	Hodges
Donahue	1	television
Doris Day: Her Own Story	1	Day

TITLE	NUMBER OF CHALLENGES	AUTHOR (BOOKS) OR FORMAT
Double Cross	1	comic
Double Spiral for a Hillside	1	art
Double Take	1	Dowling
Down by the River	1	Hunt
Dr. Ruth Westheimer	1	speech
Dragon	1	student press
Drexel Triangle	1	student newspaper
drug education books	1	textbook
Drugs from A to Z: A Dictionary	1	Lingeman
Duluth, Minnesota anti-draft speakers	1	speech
Duquesne Duke	1	student newspaper
Eagle's Cry	1	student newspaper
Eagle's Eye	1	student newspaper
Earth Science	1	textbook
East of Eden	1	Steinbeck
Easy Rider	1	magazine
Eating Disorders	1	Josephs
Edith Jackson	1	Guy
editiorial cartoon	1	student newspaper
Educational Exploration Center	1	speech
Eidos	1	magazine
El Marko	1	student newspaper
El Salvador: Another Vietnam?	1	television
Eleanor Smeal	1	speech
Elektra: Assassin	1	comic
Elvis Presley records	1	music
Emmanuelle	1	film
Emmanuelle: The Joys of a Woman	1	film
Emotions: Can You Trust Them?	1	Dobson
Emperor Jones	1	O'Neill
Emperor's Hymn- Deutschland Uber Alies	1	music
Emperor's New Clothes: Censorship, Sexuality, and the Body Politic	1	exhibit
Empire Stikes Back	1	Glut
Endless Quest	1	Sutton
Energy Consumer	1	document
English- Writing and Skills	1	textbook
entire curriculum of sex education texts	1	textbook
Epitaph	1	student newspaper
erotic art and photographs	1	art
Escapade (movie channel)	1	television
escort advertisements in yellow pages	1	advertisement
Eva J. Paterson (commencement speaker)	1	speech
Everything You Always Wanted to Know About Sex	1	Reuben
Ewoks Join the Fight	1	book
Ex-Mutants	1	comic
Exodus	1	magazine

TITLE	NUMBER OF CHALLENGES	AUTHOR (BOOKS) OR FORMAT
Experiences in Biology	1	textbook
Exploring Career Decision Making	1	textbook
Exploring Life Through Literature	1	textbook
Exploring Living Things	1	textbook
Exploring Science: K Through Grade 6	1	texbook
Exponent	1	student newspaper
Faces of Death	1	film
Faces of War	1	film
Facts of Birth	1	textbook
Fairless Union News	1	newspaper
Fallen Angels	1	Myers
Falling Bodies	1	Kaufman
Families	1	book
Family Life and Human Sexuality	1	textbook
family planning presentation	1	film
Fanfares	1	textbook
Far Cry from Yesterday	1	film
Farewell to Arms	1	Hemingway
Fast Sam, Cool Clyde and Stuff	1	Meyers
Fatal Flowers: On Sin, Sex and Suicide in the Deep South	1	Daniell
Father Andrew Greeley	1	speech
Favorite Son	1	television
FBI documents on John Lennon	1	document
Fear of Flying	1	Jong
Federal Trade Commission documents	1	documents
female nude drawing	1	art
Few Good Men	1	magazine
fifth grade vocabulary workbook	1	textbook
Fifty True Tales of Terror	1	Canning
Fighters, Refugees, Immigrants: A Tale of the Hmong	1	Goldfarb
film series on Russian opera and ballet	1	film
Find a Stranger, Say Good-bye	1	Lowry
Fixer	1	Malamud
Flashdance	1	film
Flashpoint--Israel and the Palestinians	1	television
Flint Gay Coalition dance	1	dance
Forest Park News	1	newspaper
Fort Lewis College Independent	1	student newspaper
fortune telling	1	other
forty paintings by Douglas Van Dyke	1	art
Forum	1	magazine
Fossil Record	1	film
four paintings by Elaine Good	1	art
Fragile Flag	1	Langton
Frankenchrist	1	art
Frat House	1	film

TITLE	NUMBER OF CHALLENGES	AUTHOR (BOOKS) OR FORMAT
fraternity newsletter	1	student press
Friends 'til the End	1	Strasser
Funny Thing Happened on the Way to the Forum	1	play
Galaxy	1	student newspaper
Games of Wizards	1	Ponce
Garfield: His Nine Lives	1	Davis
Gary Hodgen (federal research scientist)	1	speech
gay and lesbian speakers	1	speech
Gay Community News	1	newspaper
Gay Pride Committee advertisements	1	advertisements
Gay Report	1	Jay
Gaydreams	1	radio
Gaze	1	newspaper
Genuine Texas Handbook	1	Kent
George C. Marshall papers	1	other
Georgia Gazette	1	newspaper
Gerald Carlson (Congressional candidate)	1	speech
Get Organized	1	Fiske
Get to Know Your Rabbit	1	film
Ghostbusters	1	film
Ghosts	1	book
Gimme an H.E.L.P.	1	Bonham
Gina Cassone (author)	1	speech
Giovannis' Room	1	other
Girl Named Sooner	1	Clauser
Girl Scout sex education program	1	other
Girls and Sex	1	Pomeroy
Girls of Virginia Tech calendar	1	other
Give Me One Good Reason	1	Klein
Glamour	1	magazine
Glass Menagerie	1	Williams
Glitter Dome	1	Wambaugh
Glory and the Dream	1	Manchester
God Makers	1	Herbert
God, the Universe and Hot Fudge Sundaes	1	Howe
Godfather	1	film
Gods of Demons	1	Lightner
Good Doctor	1	play
Good Health For You	1	textbook
Goodbye, Columbus	1	Roth
Governing Your Life: Citizenship and Civics	1	textbook
Governor Baxter School for the Deaf News	1	student newspaper
Graveyard Tales	1	music
Great Expectations	1	Dickens
Great Waves are Breaking	1	book

TITLE	NUMBER OF CHALLENGES	AUTHOR (BOOKS) OR FORMAT
Green Desire	1	Myrer
Grenadier	1	student press
Grossmont High School newspaper anti-draft advertisments	1	student newspaper
Group	1	McCarthy
Growing Up	1	book
Growing Up: How We Become Alive, Born, and Grow	1	DeSchweinitz
Growth and Reproduction	1	textbook
Guess Who's Pregnant Now	1	film
Guidon	1	student newspaper
Guillermo Ungo (Salvadoran rebel leader)	1	speech
Gun in the House	1	television
H.G. Bissinger	1	speech
Hair	1	play
hairstyle and color of student Lory Margues	1	other
Halloween	1	book
Halloween: Season of the Witch	1	Martin
Handbook for Conscientious Objectors	1	Sealy
Handy Dandy Evolution Refuter	1	textbook
Hanging Out Mitti Cici	1	Pascal
Happy Birthday Planet Earth	1	book
Happy Hooker	1	film
Harbor College Hawk	1	student newspaper
Harpers	1	magazine
Harriet the Spy	1	Fitzhugh
Hatchet Job	1	student press
Haunting of America	1	Anderson
Hawk Tawk	1	student newspaper
Head Man	1	Platt
Headless Cupid	1	Snyder
Headless Horseman Rides Tonight and other Poems	1	Prelutsky
Health and Safety	1	textbook
health education course	1	other
health education curriculum	1	other
Health, A Way of Life	1	textbook
Heaven is a Playground	1	Telander
Heavy Metal	1	comic
heavy metal music	1	music
Hegira	1	student press
Help!	1	film
Herbert Armstrong's Tangled Web	1	Robinson
Herbie Capleenies	1	Bopp
Heritage	1	student newspaper
Heritage Songbook	1	textbook
Heroic Figure	1	art

TITLE	NUMBER OF CHALLENGES	AUTHOR (BOOKS) OR FORMAT
Hey, Naked Lady	1	play
high school mascot	1	other
high school valedictorian	1	speech
high school yearbook senior photograph	1	student press
Hilltop	1	student newspaper
Hippolytus	1	Eurypides
His Way: The Unauthorized Biography of Frank Sinatra	1	Kelley
History of the American Nation	1	textbook
Hit Parader	1	magazine
Hite Report on Male Sexuality	1	Hite
Holt, Rinehart texbook series	1	textbook
Holy Terror	1	film
Home Before Morning	1	VanDevanter
home economics course	1	other
Home Free	1	Murphy
homecoming float	1	other
Homosexual	1	Ebert
Honey of a Chimp	1	Klein
Hoofbeats	1	student newspaper
Hoofprint	1	student newspaper
Horizon	1	student newspaper
House Full of Kids	1	book
House Without a Christmas Tree	1	Rock
How Does it Feel? Exploring the World of Your Senses	1	book
How Was I Born?	1	Wabbes
How They Grow	1	textbook
How to Eat Fried Worms	1	Rockwell
How to Make Love to a Man	1	Penney
How You Were Born	1	Cole
Howard Stern talk radio show	1	radio
Human Body	1	book
Human Sexuality in Nursing Process	1	textbook
Human Story	1	textbook
Humorist Manifesto	1	student press
Hunger of Memory	1	textbook
Hurricane	1	student newspaper
I Dismember Mamma	1	film
I Know You Al	1	Greene
I Love You	1	film
I Spit on Your Grave	1	film
I'll Get You	1	book
I'm My Own Grandpa	1	music
ice sculpture	1	art
If Beale Street Could Talk	1	Baldwin
If There Be Thorns	1	Andrews
If You Love This Planet	1	film

TITLE	NUMBER OF CHALLENGES	AUTHOR (BOOKS) OR FORMAT
Iggie's House	1	Blume
Illini Chronicle	1	student newspaper
Illusions	1	Bach
Illustrated Encyclopedia of Family Health	1	book
Illustrated Social History of Prostitution	1	Bullough
Immigrants	1	Fast
Impact of Our Past: A History of the United States	1	textbook
In a Dark, Dark Room and Other Scary Stories	1	Schwartz
In Memoriam	1	art
In Our Own Backyards	1	film
In Our Water	1	film
In the Beginning	1	book
In the Claws of the Red Dragon	1	exhibit
In the Name of the Father	1	Quinnell
In the Rabbit's Garden	1	Lionni
Indecent Obsession	1	McCullough
Independent Press	1	student newspaper
Indiana Jones and the Temple of Doom	1	film
Inferno	1	Dante
Informer	1	student newspaper
Insatiable	1	film
Inside the Sexes	1	television
Intelligence Network	1	film
International	1	magazine
International Family Planning Perspective	1	magazine
international studies program	1	other
interview with White Plains police officer	1	radio
Introduction to Social Science	1	textbook
Intruder in the Dust	1	Faulkner
Invitation to Psychology	1	textbook
Iowa State Daily	1	student newspaper
Is There Life After High School?	1	play
Israel Calling (KQED radio program)	1	radio
It	1	King
J.D. Salinger: A Writing Life	1	Hamilton
J.T.	1	Wagner
Jackson Journal	1	student newspaper
Jan Cole	1	speech
Jan Klemp	1	speech
Jane Fonda, the Actress in Her Time	1	Guiles
Japanese sceen painting	1	art
Jaws	1	Benchley
Jay Hawker	1	student newspaper
Jerker (radio play)	1	radio
Jesse Jackson	1	speech
Jimmy Swaggart's television show	1	television

TITLE	NUMBER OF CHALLENGES	AUTHOR (BOOKS) OR FORMAT
Joe Bob Goes to the Drive-in	1	newspaper
John Bowley and John Wilson (stand-up comediens)	1	other
John Seiler	1	speech
Johnsonian	1	student newspaper
Jolly Roger	1	student newspaper
Joy of Gay Sex	1	Silverstein
Judevine	1	play
Junior Great Books program	1	other
Just Hold On	1	Bunn
Justice in America	1	textbook
K.D. Lang	1	music
Kahoki	1	student newspaper
Kansas City	1	television
Katie Morag and the Tiresome Ted	1	Hedderwick
Kid's First Book About Sex	1	Blank
Killing Fields	1	film
King Lear	1	Shakespeare
King Stork	1	Lee
Kinsman	1	Bova
Klansman	1	magazine
Klu Klux Klan	1	speech
Klu Klux Klan forum	1	speech
Knight Times	1	student newspaper
La Vaz Del Vaquero	1	student newspaper
Lace	1	Conran
Lafayette Times	1	student newspaper
Lake Breeze	1	student newspaper
Lake Worth Community High School Yearbook	1	student press
Lambda Report	1	television
Lane Kirkland (President AFL-CIO)	1	speech
Lathe of Heaven	1	LeGuin
law opinion of Judge Fred Weiner	1	document
Learning About Sex	1	Aho
Learning Tree	1	Parks
Leefried Iander photograph	1	art
Lesbian Couples	1	Green
Librol Revolution	1	other
license plate logo	1	other
Life Before Birth: The Story of the First Nine Months	1	Parker
Life of Brian	1	film
Life Science	1	textbook
Light in the Forest	1	Richter
Like a Prayer (by Madonna)	1	music
limerick anthology	1	book
Limericks: Historical and Hysterical	1	Billington

TITLE	NUMBER OF CHALLENGES	AUTHOR (BOOKS) OR FORMAT
lithographys by Kevin Kennedy	1	art
Little Abigail and the Beautiful Pony	1	other
Little Big Man	1	Berger
Little Foxes	1	Hellman
The Little Mermaid	1	film
Live Options	1	newspaper
Living Bible	1	book
Living Law series	1	textbook
Living Today	1	textbook
Log	1	student newspaper
Logan Courier	1	student newspaper
Lolita	1	play
Lonesome George and the Bushwacker	1	art
Long Beach Junior High yearbook	1	student press
Long Day's Journey Into Night	1	O'Neill
Longarm in Virginia City	1	Evans
Loon	1	student newspaper
The Lord is My Shepherd and He Knows I'm Gay	1	Perry
Los Angeles Times	1	newspaper
Lost Horizon	1	Hilton
Lou Grant	1	television
Louis Farrakhan	1	speech
Louis Polisar	1	speech
Love is One of the Choices	1	Klein
Lovesexy	1	music
Loving Sex for Both Sexes	1	Carlson
Lucky	1	comic
Lumberjack	1	student newspaper
Luna	1	film
Lutheran	1	magazine
Lynchburg Daily Advance	1	newspaper
Lynchburg News	1	newspaper
M. C. Hammer	1	music
Ma Prem Isabel (a follower of Bhagwan Shree Rajnessh)	1	speech
Macohi	1	student newspaper
Magic Circle (instructional technique)	1	other
Magical Mystery Tour	1	film
Magician	1	Stein
magician's performance	1	other
Main Street	1	television
Major British Writers	1	Harrison
Making Bacon (song)	1	radio
Male Couples Guide to Living Together	1	Marcus
Man Who Came to Dinner	1	Kaufman
Man, Myth and Magic	1	Boyd
Marcella	1	Ward

TITLE	NUMBER OF CHALLENGES	AUTHOR (BOOKS) OR FORMAT
Margaret J. Randall	1	speech
Marion McGrath (citizen at town meeting)	1	speech
Marketing Management: Text and Cases	1	textbook
Married With Children	1	television
Marxist summer institute	1	other
Mary Karasch	1	speech
Maryknoll Order of Roman Catholic Church Film	1	film
Maryland State Medical Journal	1	magazine
Masculinity and Femininity	1	textbook
Masquerade	1	Shreve
Matarese Circle	1	Ludlum
Matchmaker	1	play
Mayor of Casterbridge	1	Hardy
MCC Voice	1	student newspaper
McDougal-Littel Reading Literature series	1	textbook
McTeague	1	Norris
Me Books	1	book
Me: Understanding Myself and Others	1	textbook
Media Monopoly	1	Bagdikian
Medium	1	music
Meet the Vampire	1	McHargue
Meet the Werewolf	1	McHargue
Mein Kampf	1	Hitler
Meltdown	1	play
Men and Nations	1	text
Merchant of Venice	1	Shakespeare
Merry Wives of Windsor	1	play
Metamorphosis	1	student press
Metanoia	1	art
Metrication, American Style	1	Izzi
Miami Herald	1	newspaper
Michigan Model for Comprehensive School Health pamphlet	1	other
Mighty Mouse	1	television
Militant and Young Socialist	1	newspaper
Mistral's Daughter	1	Krantz
Mirror	1	student newspaper
Miss and Mr. Nude Indiana Pageant	1	other
Miss Julie	1	Strindberg
Mississippi Burning	1	film
Modern American History	1	textbook
Modern Sex	1	textbook
Modern Sex Education	1	textbook
Modern Witch's Handbook	1	book
Monster Madnews	1	play
Monsters and Other Science Mysteries	1	film
Montclarion and the Berkley Voice	1	newspaper

TITLE	NUMBER OF CHALLENGES	AUTHOR (BOOKS) OR FORMAT
Moon in Its Flight	1	other
More Joy of Sex	1	Comfort
Moslem Student Association literature	1	other
Mothers and Daughters, Fathers and Sons	1	exhibit
Motif	1	student newspaper
movie about a prostitute (KDKA TV)	1	television
movies	1	film
Mr. Ed	1	television
MTV	1	televsion
mural on housing project	1	art
mural on pillar in school cafeteria	1	art
Murder	1	comic
Music	1	textbook
Musical Stage Revue	1	play
Mustang Daily	1	student newspaper
Mustang Express	1	student newspaper
My Brother Sam is Dead	1	Collier
Mysterious Powers and Strange Forces	1	Humberstone
Mystery of Astrology	1	film
Mystery of ESP	1	film
Mystery of Witchcraft	1	film
Mysticism: Sacred and Profane	1	Zaehner
na-ni	1	Deveaux
Naomi in the Middle	1	Klein
Nation	1	magazine
Nation of Islam speaker	1	speech
National Vanguard	1	magazine
National Women's Studies Association conference	1	other
Native Son	1	Wright
Natural Science: Bridging the Gap	1	textbook
Navigator	1	student press
Nehdi Terzi	1	speech
Neopolitan Monthly	1	student newspaper
New Baby Comes	1	book
New Centurions	1	Wambaugh
New Directions	1	magazine
New Expressions	1	student newspaper
New Limerick	1	book
New Mexico Daily Lobo	1	student newspaper
New York Post film advertisement	1	advertisement
News Herald	1	newspaper
news report based on a soldier's diary	1	newspaper
news report on home improvement scandal	1	television
Nigger of the Narcissus	1	Conrad
Night of Fire and Blood	1	Kelley
Night Sanctuary	1	Van Vooren

TITLE	NUMBER OF CHALLENGES	AUTHOR (BOOKS) OR FORMAT
Nightmare and Armadillo (by Clyde Burnette)	1	art
Nightmares	1	Prelutsky
Nightwork	1	Shaw
Nine Stories	1	Salinger
Nineteen Eighty Four	1	Orwell
Nino Pasti (retired NATO general)	1	speech
No Place to Run	1	Tracy
No Sacred Cows	1	television
Norma Rae	1	film
North Dakota Farmer	1	magazine
Northern Illinois University erotic film festival	1	film
Norwich Bulletin	1	newspaper
Not for Profit	1	student newspaper
nude beauty pageant	1	other
nude drawings	1	art
nude photographs (by Jacqueline Livingston)	1	art
nude study for painting	1	art
Nugget	1	magazine
Occult America	1	Godwin
occult seminar	1	other
Oedipus Plays of Sophocles	1	Sophocles
Oedipus the King	1	Sophocles
Olathe Daily News	1	student newspaper
Old Brooklyn News	1	newspaper
Old Man and the Sea	1	Hemingway
On Baile's Strand	1	Yeats
On Reading Palms	1	Thomson
Once a Man Knew His Name	1	other
one biology text	1	textbook
One Day in the Life of Ivan Denisovich	1	Solzhenitsyn
One Hundred Years of Solitude	1	Garcia Marquez
One Hundredth Thing About Caroline	1	Lowry
The One in the Middle is the Green Kanagaroo	1	Blume
Opening of Misty Beethoven	1	film
Order Reigns in South Africa	1	art
OSHA booklet on cotton dust	1	document
Other	1	Tryon
Other Side of the Coin	1	Boulle
Otherwise Known as Sheila the Great	1	Blume
Our Own	1	newspaper
Our Paper	1	newspaper
Out on a Limb	1	MacLaine
Pace Press	1	student newspaper
paid ad in yearbook	1	advertisement

TITLE	NUMBER OF CHALLENGES	AUTHOR (BOOKS) OR FORMAT
painting	1	art
painting (by Bob Plageman)	1	art
painting (by Jeffrey Hull)	1	art
painting (by Mary Cate Carroll)	1	art
painting (by student David Nelson)	1	art
painting (by Trevor Southey)	1	art
painting (by Walter Coleman)	1	art
painting of Mayor Harold Washington	1	art
paintings (by Cuban artist Amelia Pelaez)	1	art
Palo Verde Post	1	student newspaper
Panther's Tale	1	student newspaper
Paragon	1	student newspaper
Parenting and Children	1	textbook
pastel drawings (by Alicia Czechowski)	1	art
Paw Prints	1	student newspaper
Peace and Nuclear Age Curriculum	1	other
peace symbol	1	other
Peachtree Preaching street preachers	1	speech
Pearl	1	Steinbeck
Pebble in Newcomb's Pond	1	Dengler
Pentagon report on harassment and discrimination	1	document
Pequonian	1	student press
performance art	1	art
Persecution and Assassination of Jean Paul Marat	1	play
person(s) and their t-shirts	1	other
Personal Adjustment: Marriage and Family Living	1	textbook
Pet Cemetery	1	King
Philip Bacuyani	1	speech
photograph exhibit for Protrait: Form and Concept	1	textbook
photograph exhibit of male nudes	1	art
photograph of nude 4-year-old child	1	art
photographic art exhibit	1	exhibit
photographs (by Starr Ockenga)	1	art
photographs by 1 artist submitted for group exhibit	1	exhibit
Pigman	1	film
The Pill Versus the Springhill Mine Disaster	1	Brautigan
Pissing in the Snow and Other Ozark Folktales	1	book
Plain Truth	1	magazine
Planned Parenthood advertisements	1	advertisements
Planned Parenthood films	1	film
Planned Parenthood sex education materials	1	other

TITLE	NUMBER OF CHALLENGES	AUTHOR (BOOKS) OR FORMAT
Planned Parenthood teacher's guide and resource manual	1	textbook
play on AIDS	1	play
Player Piano	1	Vonnegut
Player's Girl	1	magazine
Players	1	magazine
Playing for Time	1	television
Point Blank	1	student newspaper
Point of Departure	1	textbook
Polaris	1	student newspaper
policy to restrict children from non- juvenile materials	1	other
political banners	1	other
political signs	1	advertisement
Popular History of Witchcraft	1	Summers
pornographic film scheduled but not chosen	1	film
Portrait of America, Volume II	1	textbook
Possible Impossibilities	1	Hall
posters of Marx and Lenin	1	art
Powder Horn Press	1	student newspaper
press conference of a marine who fought in Grenada	1	other
Prince and the Pauper	1	Twain
Prince in Waiting	1	Christopher
Prince of Tides	1	Conroy
Princess Daisy (mini-series)	1	television
Princeton Tiger	1	student press
Princeton University band	1	music
Private Lessons	1	film
Professor J.D. Martin	1	speech
Professor Jeffrey Richelson	1	speech
Progressive	1	magazine
Prom Night	1	television
Prometheus Unbound	1	Shelley
promotional poster	1	art
proof sheet	1	art
protestor against CIA	1	other
protestor who burned a U.S. flag	1	other
psychic art fair	1	other
Psychic Stories Strange But True	1	Atkinson
Psychology: Exploring Behavior	1	textbook
PTA Newsletter	1	other
public access cable TV program	1	television
Public Assistance: Why Bother Working for a Living	1	game
public dancing	1	dance
Public Enemy	1	music

TITLE	NUMBER OF CHALLENGES	AUTHOR (BOOKS) OR FORMAT
public relations packet commemorating D-Day	1	other
public service announcement on teenage pregnancy	1	advertisement
Public Smiles, Private Tears	1	VanSlyke
Purple Press	1	student newspaper
Pushcart War	1	play
Quad	1	student newspaper
Queen of What Ifs	1	Klein
Quest	1	student newspaper
Quickie	1	film
Rabbit Run	1	Updike
Radical Establishment	1	student newspaper
radio advertisements for Arab-American group	1	advertisement
radio advertisement	1	advertisement
radio station slogan	1	radio
Raider Review	1	student newspaper
Rainbow Jordan	1	student newspaper
Raisin in the Sun	1	Hansberry
Ralph Nader	1	speech
Rape: The Bait and the Trap	1	MacKeller
Reading Fiction	1	textbook
records, cassettes, videos, posters, books	1	other
Red Badge of Courage	1	Crane
Red Sky at Morning	1	Bradford
Redbook	1	magazine
Relationships: A Study in Human Behavior	1	textbook
Religious Herald	1	newspaper
Remar Sutton	1	radio
Remember Me When This You See	1	Morrison
Reproductive System: How Living Creatures Multiply	1	Silverstein
Responsive Parenting	1	textbook
Return to Oz	1	film
Reverend Charles E. Curran	1	speech
Reverend Motalepula Chabaku	1	speech
Richards Herald	1	student newspaper
Riders on the Earth	1	Weiss
Right On!	1	magazine
right to life materials	1	other
Rights of Gay People	1	ACLU
Rigoletto	1	music
Riley Review	1	student newspaper
Rio Miranda	1	student newspaper
Rita	1	music
Robert Mapplethorpe: The Perfect Moment	1	exhibit

TITLE	NUMBER OF CHALLENGES	AUTHOR (BOOKS) OR FORMAT
Robert Rutka (reporter for Prensa Latina Canada LTD)	1	other
Robert Swoboda (citizen of St. Louis)	1	speech
rock and roll music in the classroom	1	music
rock and roll records	1	music
Rock Hall of Fame	1	textbook
Rocky Horror Picture Show	1	film
Rocky Mountain High	1	music
Rolling Harvey Down the Hill	1	Prelutsky
Rolling Stone Illustrated History of Rock and Roll	1	book
Roots of Disbelief	1	film
Rosemary Curb and Nancy Manahan	1	speech
Roughrider	1	student newspaper
Ruben Zamora (Nicaraguan leftist)	1	speech
Runaways	1	play
Running Loose	1	book
Ruth Hill (author of Hanto Yo)	1	speech
Salo--The 120 Days of Sodom	1	film
Sammy and Rosie Get Laid	1	film
San Francisco Gay Men's Choir concert	1	music
Sapphistry: The Book of Lesbian Sexuality	1	Califia
Sarah Weddington	1	speech
Satanists	1	Haining
Scholastic Tribune	1	student newspaper
school mascot	1	other
school TV news program	1	television
Science Editor	1	radio
Scope English Program	1	textbook
Scott House (male stripper)	1	dance
Screaming Eagle	1	student newspaper
sculpture by Billy Lawless and Kathie Simonds	1	art
Second Coming	1	comic
Second Generation	1	East
Secrecy and Democracy: CIA in Transition	1	Turner
Secret Agent	1	film
Seduction	1	book
Seduction of Joe Tynan	1	film
Self	1	book
Sense of Honor	1	Webb
Serpico	1	Maas
Servants of the Devil	1	Aylesworth
seven paintings (various artists)	1	art
Seven Theories of Human Nature	1	Stevenson
Seventeen	1	television

TITLE	NUMBER OF CHALLENGES	AUTHOR (BOOKS) OR FORMAT
Seventh East Press	1	student newspaper
seventh grade science textbook	1	textbook
several paintings (by Dan Gustin)	1	art
several photographs (by Robin Milsom)	1	art
sex and values education program	1	other
Sex Atlas	1	Haeberle
sex education and health tapes	1	other
Sex, Drugs, and AIDS	1	film
Sex, Sexuality and You	1	Cooney
Sex-A-Peel-A-Gram yellow pages advertisment	1	advertisement
Sex: Telling It Straight	1	Johnson
Sexual Solutions: An Informative Guide	1	Castleman
Sexuality: A Responsible Approach	1	textbook
Shadow box	1	play
Shaka-Zulu	1	television
shanty protesting South African apartheid	1	other
Sharkey's Machine	1	Diehl
shirt (worn by James Mills)	1	other
Sidewalk Story	1	textbook
Silent Night, Deadly Night	1	film
Silent Scream	1	film
Simpsons	1	television
Simpsons (and other) t-shirts	1	other
Sioux City, Past and Present	1	textbook
Sir Gawain and the Loathly Lady	1	Hastings
Sixty Minutes	1	television
sketch (by Douglas Eskra)	1	art
Skim	1	Henege
Snow Bound	1	Mazer
Social Studies	1	textbook
Sociology: The Search for Social Patterns	1	textbook
Sol Gordon	1	speech
Soldier Girls	1	film
Solitary Secret	1	Hermes
Songs and Stories of the Netsik Eskimos	1	textbook
Sons and Lovers	1	television
Sorcerer and Friends	1	play
Soul on Ice	1	Cleaver
Soup	1	Peck
Soup and Me	1	Peck
South Shore Record	1	newspaper
Spaced Out	1	film
Spectator	1	newspaper
Spelling: Words and Skills	1	textbook
Spice	1	student press
Spin	1	magazine
Spiral Dance	1	Garcia y Robinson

TITLE	NUMBER OF CHALLENGES	AUTHOR (BOOKS) OR FORMAT
Spirit of Hoover	1	art
Split Second	1	play
Sports Illustrated	1	magazine
Spotlight	1	magazine
St. John's Passion	1	music
Stag	1	magazine
Stage Brat	1	Terris
stained glass pictures of Lysistrata	1	art
Stan Freburg's Federal Budget Review	1	television
Stand	1	King
Standing Figure Frame (sculpture)	1	art
Star Witness	1	Kluger
Stars	1	magazine
Stars and Stripes	1	newspaper
Stars, Spells, Secrets and Sorcery	1	Haislip
state approved textbooks	1	textbook
State of Grace	1	Pentauro
Stepfather	1	Reichman
Steppenwolf	1	Hesse
Stern	1	magazine
still life with skull, vidalia onions and tools	1	art
Sting	1	student newspaper
Stoney Burke (street satirist)	1	speech
Stop Rape! (student sculpture)	1	art
Story of Passover for Children	1	Silberg
Strange Case of Dr. Jekyl and Mr. Hyde	1	Stevenson
Stripes	1	film
Strong-Willed Child	1	Dobson
student attire similar to Michael Jackson	1	other
Student Bodies	1	film
Harvir Grewal(student)	1	speech
student mural	1	art
student mural of the rock group Kiss	1	art
student political rally	1	other
student produced flyers and pamphlets	1	other
student produced paintings	1	art
student survey on alcohol and drug use	1	other
student yearbook	1	student press
Stupids Step Out	1	Allard
Sugar Walls	1	music
Suicide's Wife	1	Madden
Summer to Die	1	Lowry
The Sun Also Rises	1	Hemingway
Sun City	1	television
Sunday morning church service broadcast	1	television
Super Teen	1	magazine
Superstars of Rock	1	textbook
Survival Series	1	textbook

TITLE	NUMBER OF CHALLENGES	AUTHOR (BOOKS) OR FORMAT
Swank	1	magazine
Sword and Shield	1	student newspaper
The Sword and the Sorcerer	1	film
t-shirt	1	other
t-shirt (Experts Agree! Meese is a Pig)	1	other
t-shirt (with Christian Rock group Stryper)	1	other
t-shirts (dealing with drugs, alcohol, obesity and violence)	1	other
Table Settings	1	play
Taboo	1	film
Taliypo	1	Galdone
Taking Care of Terrific	1	Lowry
Tale Blazer Library	1	book
talk radio show (on WAVI)	1	radio
talk radio program (William Gale and James Wickstrom)	1	radio
Tall Men From Boston	1	book
Tartar Shield	1	student newspaper
Tarzan, the Apeman	1	film
Tattoo	1	film
technical papers at Symposium of Photo-Optical Engineers	1	other
Teen Wolf	1	film
Teenage Body Book	1	Wibblesman
Tell it to the King	1	King
Terrorism and Democracy	1	Turner
Texas Chainsaw Massacre	1	film
Texas Review	1	student newspaper
Texas, U.S. and the World	1	textbook
textbook series	1	textbook
Then One Year	1	film
Therese Racquin	1	television
thirteen gay books and publications	1	book
This Badge Means You	1	music
This is Judy Woodruff at the White House	1	Woodruff
This Note's for You	1	music
Those Young Girls	1	film
Thousand Pieces of Gold	1	McCunn
Three Billy Goats Gruff	1	book
Three Comedies of American Life	1	Mersand
Three Hundred Sixty Five Days	1	Glasser
three paintings	1	art
three photographs by Patti Dobson	1	art
three student paintings	1	art
Tiger Beat	1	magazine
Tiger Times	1	student newspaper
Tiger's Tale	1	student newspaper
Tilted Arc (by Richard Serra)	1	art

TITLE	NUMBER OF CHALLENGES	AUTHOR (BOOKS) OR FORMAT
Tim Mayer (Israeli graduate student)	1	speech
Time Magazine	1	magazine
Tiny Tim	1	Oxenburg
Tip on a Dead Crab	1	Murray
Titan Times	1	student newspaper
title/ author not given	1	book
To See Ourselves	1	book
Today's Teen	1	textbook
Toilet	1	play
Tomas Borge (Nicaraguan Interior Minister)	1	speech
Tony Awards show	1	television
topless male jogger	1	other
Torso	1	magazine
Tour de Farce	1	student newspaper
Tower Times	1	student newspaper
Towne Crier	1	student newspaper
Treasury of American Poetry	1	book
Trig	1	Peck
Truly Tasteless Jokes	1	Knott
Truth in Crisis: The Controversy in the Southern Baptist Convention	1	book
Twelfth Night	1	Shakespeare
Twin Cities Reader	1	newspaper
two anti-Reagan posters	1	art
Two Live Crew concert	1	music
two murals (by Michael Spafford)	1	art
two paintings	1	art
two paintings (by Beth Stevens)	1	art
two paintings (by William Klenk)	1	art
two poems ("Hist Whist" & "The Hay")	1	other
Tyrsis	1	student press
U.N. conference on non-governmental organizations	1	other
U.S. Department of Education Newsletter	1	document
Uncle Tom's Cabin	1	Stowe
Underground	1	student newspaper
Understanding Your Parents	1	textbook
Underwater	1	student newspaper
Unicorns in the Rain	1	Cohen
Unidentified Flying Objects	1	Asimov
Union	1	student newspaper
United Methodist Reporter	1	advertisement
United States and the Middle East	1	textbook
University Times	1	student newspaper
university yearbook	1	student press
Up in Seth's Room	1	Mazer
Upchuck Summer	1	Schwartz

TITLE	NUMBER OF CHALLENGES	AUTHOR (BOOKS) OR FORMAT
Urban Cowboy	1	film
Urban Guerrillas	1	music
Using English, First	1	textbook
Vacavalley Star	1	newspaper
valedictorian speech (by Lizette Espana)	1	speech
Valley Echo	1	student newspaper
Values Clarification	1	textbook
values clarification class	1	other
van with nude artwork painted on exterior	1	art
vanity license plate	1	other
various rap, comedy and heavy metal recordings	1	music
various recordings	1	radio
various textbooks	1	textbook
Victor/ Victoria	1	film
videos depicting violence	1	film
videotapes in general	1	film
View from Another Closet	1	Bade
View from the Cherry Tree	1	Roberts
Visions of the Future: Magic Boards	1	Stadtmauer
Visitor	1	newspaper
Vista	1	student newspaper
Vixen	1	film
Vladimir Bakhurov (Soviet Vice Consul)	1	speech
vocabulary book	1	textbook
Vocational Home Economics for Family Living	1	textbook
Vogue	1	magazine
wall mural	1	art
War on Villa Street	1	Mazer
War Year	1	Haldeman
Washburn High School alternative student newspaper	1	student newspaper
Washington Journal of Sex and Politics	1	magazine
Washington Times film review	1	newspaper
Waste Paper	1	student newspaper
Watermelon Song	1	music
Watership Down	1	Adams
Wee Wisdom	1	magazine
Weekly Scene	1	newspaper
western novel (title unknown)	1	book
What Does the X Mean?	1	play
What Friends are For	1	film
What Happened to Mr. Foster?	1	Bargar
What's It All About?	1	Caine
What Joy Awaits You	1	textbook
What's Happening to Me?	1	Maule

TITLE	NUMBER OF CHALLENGES	AUTHOR (BOOKS) OR FORMAT
What's Happening to My Body? Book for Boys	1	textbook
What's Happening to My Body? Book for Girls	1	textbook
When the Sky Began to Roar	1	Bach
Where Did I Come From?	1	Mahle
Where Has Deedie Wooster Been All These Years	1	Jacobs
Where's Waldo?	1	Handford
Whittier Miscellany	1	student newspaper
Whoreson	1	Goines
Wilted	1	Kropp
Windup	1	student press
Winnie the Witch	1	film
Winterset	1	book
Witches and Witchcraft	1	Hicks
Witches of Worm	1	Snyder
Witches for Hire	1	television
Wiz	1	film
Wizards	1	game
Woman's Body: An Owner's Body	1	Diagram Group Staff
Woman's Guide to a Safe Abortion	1	Corsaro
Women and Wallace	1	play
Wonderful Story of How You Were Born	1	Gruenberg
Wonderful Tonight	1	music
Word is Out	1	film
Words of Conscience: Religious Statements on Conscientious Objection	1	book
workshop on homosexuality	1	other
World History of a Golden Age	1	textbook
WQCS-PBS news	1	television
Wrinkle in Time	1	L'Engle
Wuthering Heights	1	Bronte
x-rated films	1	film
x-rated television films	1	television
yearbook cover art	1	student press
Yellow Submarine	1	film
Yes! The Annunciation (sculpture)	1	art
Yosemite Artists in Residence show	1	exhibit
You and Your Family	1	Moore
Young Miss	1	magazine
Young, Gay and Proud	1	Alyson
Your Health and Your Future	1	textbook
Your Side	1	student newspaper
Zardoc	1	film
Zodiac and Swastika	1	Wulff
Zork: The Malifesto Quest	1	Meretsky
Zsuxanna Budapest	1	speech

TITLE	NUMBER OF CHALLENGES	AUTHOR (BOOKS) OR FORMAT
ATTACKS ON THE FREEDOM TO LEARN		
Catcher in the Rye	8	Salinger
Impressions	6	textbook
Chocolate War	5	Cormier
Cujo	5	King
Go Ask Alice	5	Anonymous
Romeo and Juliet	5	Film/Play
Blubber	4	Blume
Curses, Hexes, and Spells	4	Cohen
Forever	4	Blume
Of Mice and Men	4	Steinbeck
Deenie	3	Blume
Halloween ABC	3	Merriam
I Am the Cheese	3	Cormier
I Know Why the Caged Bird Sings	3	Angelou
Servants of the Devil	3	Aylesworth
Sports Illustrated	3	Magazine
Then Again Maybe I Won't	3	Blume
Adventures of Huckleberry Finn	2	Twain
Christine	2	King
Color Purple	2	Walker
Eye of the Needle	2	Follette
Flowers for Algernon	2	Keyes
Humanities, Cultural Roots & Continuity	2	Textbook
It's Ok if You Don't Love Me	2	Klein
Little Red Riding Hood	2	Book
Merriam-Webster College Dictionary	2	Book
My Brother Sam is Dead	2	Collier
Night of Fire and Blood	2	Kelley
Ordinary People	2	Guest
Pumsey in the Pursuit of Excellence	2	Other
Runaways	2	Play
Shining	2	King
Stand	2	King
Tiger Eyes	2	Blume
To Kill a Mockingbird	2	Lee
10 Health, Phys. Ed, Home Ec., Etc. Texts	1	textbooks
100 Years of Solitude	1	Garcia Marquez
11th and 12th Semantics Class	1	Other
19 Books with references to witchcraft	1	Book
700 Rock Albums, Singles & Tapes	1	Music
85 Tests	1	Other
A...My Name Is Alice	1	Play
ABC-The Museun of Modern Art	1	Mayer
About David	1	Pfieffer
Ads for Youth Group	1	Student Newspaper
Advocate	1	Magazine
After the End	1	Lane

TITLE	NUMBER OF CHALLENGES	AUTHOR (BOOKS) OR FORMAT
AIDS Pamphlet	1	Other
AIDS: The Facts	1	Langone
Albert H. Hawkins- The Naughtiest Boy	1	Dickens
Albert H. Hawkins and the Space Rocket	1	Dickens
All God's Children Had Wings	1	Other
Alligator River	1	Other
And No Birds Sang	1	Wagner
And They Dance Real Slow in Jackson	1	Play
Angel Dust Blues	1	Strasser
Article in High School Paper	1	Student Newspaper
Articles on Sex Education	1	Student Newspaper
Articles on Teenage Pregnancy and Divorce	1	Student Newspaper
Aspects of Sex Education Unit	1	Other
Bad Seed	1	March
Beggar Man, Thief	1	Book
Being Born	1	Kitzinger
Bible	1	Book
Bible Study Classes in Public Schools	1	Other
Biloxi Blues	1	Film
Biography of Doris Day	1	Book
Biology	1	Textbook
Black Cat	1	Other
Black is Brown is Tan	1	Adoff
Black South African Speaker	1	Speech
Bless the Beasts and Children	1	Swarthout
Bloods: An Oral History of the Vietnam War by Black Veterens	1	Terry
Bon Bons and Other Passions	1	Play
Book Covers by Planned Parenthood	1	Other
Books by Klein, Blume, & Wells	1	Books
Books by Roth, Hersey, Wolfe and Records	1	Book
Books by Ursula Leguin	1	LeGuin
Books on the Occult	1	Book
Boys and Sex	1	Pomeroy
Boys Have Feelings, Too	1	Carlson
Brave New World	1	Huxley
Breaking Up	1	Brown
California Suite	1	Play
Came A Spider	1	Levy
Campfire Stories	1	Foracy
Cartoon on Moral Majority	1	Student Newspaper
Cerebus	1	Sim
Changing Bodies, Changing Lives	1	Bell
Children's Story	1	Play
Choices	1	Other
Chorus Line	1	Play
Clockwork Orange	1	Burggess
Cold Sassy Tree	1	Burns

TITLE	NUMBER OF CHALLENGES	AUTHOR (BOOKS) OR FORMAT
Comprehensive Model for School Health education	1	Other
Cornerstone Theatre Company	1	Other
Day After	1	Film
Day No Pigs Would Die	1	Peck
Dear America: Letters Home from Vietnam	1	Film
Developing Responsible Relationships	1	Merki
Developing Understanding of Self & Others	1	Other
Devil Comes To Church	1	Book
Devils and Demons	1	Book
Different Seasons	1	King
Dr. Sol Gordon on Self-Esteem	1	Speech
Drug and Alcohol Abuse Preventive program	1	Other
Drug Prevention Course - Elementary	1	Other
East of Eden	1	Steinbeck
Edith Jackson	1	Guy
Education in Sexuality	1	Other
El Norte	1	Film
Endless Quest Series	1	Sutton
Enoch	1	Other
Excalibur	1	Film
Fahrenheit 451	1	Play
Fame	1	Play
Family Relations Supplemental Material	1	Other
Far From Shore	1	Majar
Fighters, Refugees, Immigrants: A Story of	1	Goldfarb
Finding My Way	1	Rikar
Firestarter	1	King
First Born	1	Carroll
Football Dreams	1	Guy
Four Seasons	1	Film
Fragile Unions	1	Play
Freddy's Book	1	Neufeld
Fridays	1	Gauch
Full Circle	1	Steele
Geography, Civics, Etc. Texts	1	Textbooks
Girl Named Sooner	1	Book
Grease	1	Play
Grendel	1	Gardner
Guidance and Counseling Program	1	Other
Halloween Celebration	1	Other
Harlan County	1	Film
Head Man	1	Platt
Health and Home Economics Texts	1	Textbook
Health and Sexual Education Video Series	1	Film
Hearts and Minds	1	Film
Here's Looking At You, Two	1	Other

TITLE	NUMBER OF CHALLENGES	AUTHOR (BOOKS) OR FORMAT
High School Student Newspaper	1	Student Newspaper
Honey of a Chimp	1	Klein
Hoops	1	Myers
Horror of High Ride	1	Book
Human Reference Books	1	Book
Humanities, Cultural Roots and Continuities	1	Textbook
I Am Special	1	Other
I'm Mad At You	1	Cole
If Beale Street Could Talk	1	Baldwin
Illustrated Encyclopedia of Family Health	1	Book
Illustration in Textbook	1	Textbook
Impressions	1	Other
Impressions	1	Student Newspaper
In the Night Kitchen	1	Sandak
In the Rabbit Garden	1	Lionni
In This House Scott Is My Brother	1	Adler
Inherit the Wind	1	Film
Introduction to Social Science	1	Textbook
It's Not the End of the World	1	Blume
It's Not What You Expect	1	Klein
Jewelry, Clothing, Symbols Related to Satanism	1	Other
Joy of Sex	1	Comfort
Just Hold On	1	Bunn
Key to Rebecca	1	Follett
Killing Fields	1	Film
Koyaanisqatsi	1	Music
Lady Chatterly's Lover	1	Film
Leaflets and Advertising in High School Yearbooks	1	Advertisements
Learning Tree	1	Parks
Lesson On Meditation	1	Other
Life	1	Magazine
Life Out of Balance	1	Film
Literature: An Introduction To Reading & Writing	1	Book
Little Abigail and the Beautiful Pony	1	Other
Little Red Riding Hood: Retold and Illustrated	1	Book
Living Room	1	Book
Lord of the Flies	1	Golding
Macbeth	1	Film
Mad Scientist	1	Rosenbloom
Magic and the Meaning of Vodoo	1	Christensen
Magic Cauldron	1	O'Connell
Make the Most of a Good Thing, You!	1	Shaw
Marat-Sade	1	Play
Martian Chronicles	1	Bradbury

TITLE	NUMBER OF CHALLENGES	AUTHOR (BOOKS) OR FORMAT
Matarese Circle	1	Ludlum
Material About Conscientious Objectors	1	Other
Meditation Imagery, Muscle Relaxation, Breathing	1	Other
Merriam-Webster New Collegiate Dictionary	1	Book
Metamusic	1	Music
Metaphysics in Adult Education Course	1	Other
Metrication, Amercian Style	1	Magazine
Ministers Preaching Creationism	1	Other
Mistral's Daughter	1	Krantz
Monologues: Women II	1	Book
More Joy of Sex	1	Comfort
Movie on Vietnam	1	Film
My Darling, My Hamburger	1	Zindel
My Name is Davey - I'm an Alcoholic	1	Book
na-ni	1	Deceaux
Never Cry Wolf	1	Mowat
Night Chills	1	Koontz
Nightwatch	1	Play
Nightwork	1	Shaw
No Room at the Inn	1	Play
Not for Profit	1	Student Newspaper
Odd Couple	1	Play
Of Mice and Men	1	Steinbeck
Of Mice and Men	1	Play
One Flew Over the Cuckoo's Nest	1	Film
Ordinary People	1	Guest
People	1	Magazine
PG & R Rated Movies	1	Film
Phonics Book	1	Textbook
Pill Versus Spring Hill Mine Disaster	1	Brautigan
Poems of One Line or Longer	1	Book
Preventing Teen Pregnancy	1	Film
Protective Behavior	1	Other
Quartzite Trip	1	Hogan
Queen of What Ifs	1	Klein
Read About Pollution	1	Breiter
Records, Cassettes of Rock and Country Music	1	Music
Relaxation Tapes for New Age and Far East Religion	1	Music
Revolting Rhymes	1	Dahl
Revolution in Central America	1	Textbook
Rolling Harvey Down the Hill	1	Pelutsky
Rolling Stone	1	Magazine
Roxanne	1	Film
Runaways	1	Play

TITLE	NUMBER OF CHALLENGES	AUTHOR (BOOKS) OR FORMAT
Salem's Lot	1	King
Science Curriculum with Creationism	1	Other
See Texas and Die	1	Logan
Sex Ed Curriculum Based on The Great Body Shop	1	Other
Sex - Education Curriculum	1	Other
Sisters Impossible	1	Landis
Skill For Growing	1	West
Smart Enough to Know	1	Gauge
Snowman	1	Book
Solitary Secret	1	Hermes
Sorcerer's and Friends	1	Play
Stand and Other Stephen King Books	1	King
Star Witness	1	Kluger
Starring Sally J. Freeman as Herself	1	Blume
Sun Signs: The Starts in Your Life	1	Shapiro
Stars, Spells, Secrets, and Sorcery	1	Haislip
Structure of Your Body	1	Baldwin
Summer of '42	1	Raucher
Sun Also Rises	1	Hemingway
Tactics for Thinking	1	Other
Talking With Your Teenager	1	Bell
Texts of Business, Driver Ed., Language, Music	1	Textbook
Thing at the Foot of the Bed	1	Leach
Thrasher	1	Magazine
To Take a Dare	1	Dragonwagon
Tolerance Day	1	Speech
Too Much Too Soon	1	Briskin
Toward Affective Development	1	Other
Tower of Babel	1	Other
Tribes- Part of Substance Abuse Prevention	1	Other
Tuck Everlasting	1	Babbitt
Valley of the Horses	1	Auel
Values and Sex Education Courses	1	Other
Vanities	1	Play
Vision Quest	1	Davis
Visions of the Future: Palm Reading	1	Hoffman
Warren: A True Story	1	Play
Wart Son of Toad	1	Carter
Way of Love, A Way of Life	1	Hankel
Webster's Intermediate Edition Dictionary	1	Book
What's Happening to Me?	1	Mayle
Winner All the Way	1	Goudge
Winning	1	Brancato
Witches	1	Dahl
Witches' Children	1	Clapp
Witches' Handbook	1	Tindall

TITLE	NUMBER OF CHALLENGES	AUTHOR (BOOKS) OR FORMAT
Wizards	1	Game
Working	1	Terkel
Yoga Exercises in Comparative Philosophy Class	1	Other
Your Immune System	1	Nourse
Zeralda's Ogre	1	Ungerer
CENSORSHIP NEWS		
Then Again, Maybe I Won't	1	Blume
Deenie	1	Blume
365 Days	1	Book
6 books by Stephen King	1	King
9 books from school libraries	1	Book
Ads from Central Comm. for Conscientious Objectors	1	Advertisement
Are You There God? It's Me Margaret	1	Blume
Arts Focus	1	Student Publication
As I Lay Dying	1	Faulkner
Blubber	1	Blume
Brave New World	1	Huxley
Catcher In the Rye	1	Salinger
Chocolate War	1	Cormier
Confessions of Nat Turner	1	Styron
Dimensions in Life	1	Textbook
Edith Jackson	1	Guy
Family Matters	1	Textbook
Grendel	1	Gardner
I'm Mad At You	1	Cole
Inherit the Wind	1	film
Jib	1	Student Publication
Just Hold On	1	Bunn
Justice in America	1	Textbook
Lineage and Other Stories	1	Lozoff
Lottery	1	Film
Lysistrata	1	Textbook
Me: Understanding Myself & Others	1	Textbook
Merriam-Webster Collegiate Dictionary	1	Book
Miller's Tale	1	Textbook
Person to Person	1	Textbook
Publications whose ads contradict Catholic doctrine	1	Advertisements
Reviews of Mississippi Burning & Rain Man	1	Student Newspaper
Salem's Lot	1	King
Shining	1	King
Sisters Impossible	1	Landis
Way of Life, A Way of Love: A Young Person's Introduction	1	Hankel
What is a Girl? What is a Boy?	1	Waxman

TITLE	NUMBER OF CHALLENGES	AUTHOR (BOOKS) OR FORMAT
Young & Black in America	1	Alexander

STUDENT PRESS LAW CENTER REPORT		
Issues and Answers	4	Other
Salem State College Log	3	Student Newspaper
Bear Facts	2	Student
NewspaperCampus News	2	Student Newspaper
Daily Reveille	2	Student Newspaper
Heavy metal music	2	Music
South End	2	Student Newspaper
Spectator	2	Student Newspaper
Stylus	2	Student News./Yearbook
7th East Press	1	Student Alternative Press
Accuracy in Academia Newsletter	1	Other
Alestle	1	Student Newspaper
Arlington High School Yearbook	1	Yearbook
Arrow	1	Student Newspaper
Arts Focus	1	Literary Magazine
Aztec Press	1	Student Newspaper
Bad Astr	1	Student Altrernative Press
Banners	1	Speech
Bark	1	Student Newspaper
Beacon	1	Student Newspaper
Bear Facts	1	Student Newspaper
Beating the Odds	1	Yearbook
Blarney Stone	1	Student Newspaper
Bowie High School Yearbook	1	Yearbook
Bowling Green High School Newspaper	1	Student Newspaper
Bull Dog Barker	1	Student Newspaper
Cabinet	1	Student Newspaper
Cadaver	1	Other
Camel Tracks	1	Student Newspaper
Campus News	1	Student Newspaper
Campus Vigion	1	Student Newspaper
Cardozo Law Forum	1	Student Newspaper
Catonsville Times	1	Student Newspaper
Chanticleer	1	Student Newspaper
Chief Events	1	Student Newspaper
Chimas	1	Student Newspaper
Christian Pamphlets	1	Other
Chronicle	1	Student Newspaper
Clarion	1	Student Newspaper
Clarion Call	1	Student Newspaper
Clark County (Nevada) High School Student Newspapers	1	Student Newspaper
Clipper Courier	1	Student Newspaper
Colley Crossfire	1	Student Alternative Press
Common Lives/Lesbian Lives	1	Literary Magazine

TITLE	NUMBER OF CHALLENGES	AUTHOR (BOOKS) OR FORMAT
Cougar Review	1	Student Newspaper
Courier	1	Student Newspaper
Crossroads	1	Student Newspaper
Crow's Nest	1	Student Newspaper
Cue	1	Other
Daily Athenaeum	1	Student Newspaper
Daily Aztec	1	Student Newspaper
Daily Bruin	1	Student Newspaper
Daily Iowan	1	Student Newspaper
Daily Lobo	1	Student Newspaper
Daily Lobos	1	Student Newspaper
Daily Nebraskan	1	Student Newspaper
Daily Pennsylvanian	1	Student Newspaper
Daily Sundial	1	Student Newspaper
Daily Tarheel	1	Student Newspaper
Dartmouth Review	1	Student Alternative Press
DePaulia	1	Student Newspaper
Devil's Advocate	1	Student Newspaper
Dodger	1	Student Newspaper
Dragon	1	Yearbook
Duquesne duke	1	Student Newspaper
Eagle's Cry	1	Student Newspaper
Eagle's Eye	1	Student Newspaper
El Marko	1	Student Alternative Press
Epitaph	1	Student Newspaper
Erie Square Gazette	1	Student Newspaper
Exponent	1	Student Newspaper
Falcon Times	1	Student Newspaper
Fairview High School Yearbook	1	Yearbook
Florida Review	1	Student Alternative Press
Fraternity Flyer	1	Other
Green Years	1	Yearbook
Green and Gold	1	Student Newspaper
Grenadier	1	Yearbook
Harbor Hawk	1	Student Newspaper
Hatchet Job	1	Student Alternative Press
Hawk Talk	1	Student Newspaper
Herald	1	Student Newspaper
Hickman High School Magazine	1	Other
Hilltop	1	Student Newspaper
Hoofbeats	1	Student Newspaper
Horizon	1	Student Newspaper
Hornet Voice	1	Student Newspaper
Hoya	1	Student Newspaper
Humorist Manifesto	1	Student Alternative Press
Hurricane Watch	1	Student Newspaper
IHS Press	1	Student Newspaper
Ice Cream Socialist	1	Student Alternative Press

TITLE	NUMBER OF CHALLENGES	AUTHOR (BOOKS) OR FORMAT
Idaho Argonaut	1	Student Newspaper
Igmuzzi	1	Student Newspaper
Ignatian	1	Yearbook
Illini Chronicle	1	Student Alternative Press
Independence (spoof issue renamed the Incredible)	1	Student Newspaper
Independent Student News	1	Student Alternative Press
Indian Leader	1	Student Newspaper
Indiana Statesman	1	Student Newspaper
Inflight	1	Student Newspaper
Iowa State Daily	1	Student Newspaper
Jabberwocky	1	Other
Jacket Journal	1	Student Newspaper
Jackson Journal	1	Student Newspaper
Jay Talk (on KJHK)	1	Other
Jefferson Davis High School Yearbook	1	Yearbook
Jet Jotter	1	Student Newspaper
Jib	1	Literary Magazine
Juggler	1	Art Magazine
KSMS-TV News program	1	Other
Kahoki	1	Student Newspaper
Knight Times	1	Student Newspaper
Knightlife	1	Student Newspaper
Konah	1	Student Newspaper
La Voz del Vaquero	1	Student Newspaper
Lafeyette Times	1	Student Newspaper
Langham Creek High School Yearbook	1	Yearbook
Lincolnian	1	Student Newspaper
Lion's Voice	1	Student Newspaper
Lodestar	1	Literary Magazine
Long Beach Union	1	Student Alternative Press
Loon	1	Student Alternative Press
Lumberjack	1	Student Newspaper
Mariner	1	Yearbook
Maroon	1	Student Newspaper
Marquette Tribune	1	Student Newspaper
Michigan State News	1	Student Newspaper
Mirror	1	Student Newspaper
Montana Kaiman	1	Student Newspaper
Morning Call	1	Student Newspaper
Motif	1	Art Magazine
Mountaineer Weekly	1	Student Newspaper
Nelphian	1	Student Newspaper
New Expression	1	Other
New Morning	1	Student Newspaper
New University	1	Student Newspaper
Nickensonian	1	Student Newspaper
Norse Star	1	Student Newspaper

TITLE	NUMBER OF CHALLENGES	AUTHOR (BOOKS) OR FORMAT
Norseman's Hammer	1	Student Alternative Press
Northern Star	1	Student Newspaper
Not For Profit	1	Student Alternative Press
Off the Press	1	Student Newspaper
Ohlone Monitor	1	Student Newspaper
Orient	1	Student Newspaper
Out!	1	Student Newspaper
Owl	1	Other
Pacar Times	1	Student Newspaper
Pace Press	1	Student Newspaper
Panther Prowl	1	Student Newspaper
Paper Lion	1	Student Newspaper
Paragon	1	Student Newspaper
Parthenon	1	Student Newspaper
Patriot Pride	1	Student Newspaper
Paw Prints	1	Student Newspaper
Pendulum	1	Student Newspaper
Pioneer Press	1	Student Newspaper
Point Blank	1	Student Alternative Press
Polaris	1	Student Newspaper
Politician	1	Yearbook
Poly Post	1	Student Newspaper
Pork Dukes, rock group	1	Other
Post	1	Student Newspaper
Poster	1	Art Magazine
Potrero Hill Beat	1	Other
Powder Horn Press	1	Student Newspaper
Prairie	1	Student Newspaper
Princeton University band half-time show	1	Other
Progressive rock and roll music	1	Other
Promethean	1	Student Newspaper
Purple Press	1	Student Newspaper
Purple and Gray	1	Student Newspaper
Radio Talk Show on Liberty University student radio station	1	Other
Raider Review	1	Student Newspaper
Ratical	1	Student Alternative Press
Record	1	Student Newspaper
Reflections	1	Literary Magazine
Review	1	Student Newspaper
Rio Mirada	1	Student Newspaper
Rotunda	1	Yearbook
Sagamore	1	Student Newspaper
Scholastic	1	Literary Magazine
Scholastic Tribune	1	Student Newspaper
Scroll	1	Student Newspaper
Seminole Collegian	1	Student Newspaper
Seniorities	1	Student Alternative Press

TITLE	NUMBER OF CHALLENGES	AUTHOR (BOOKS) OR FORMAT
Setonian	1	Student Newspaper
Silver Quill	1	Student Newspaper
Snapper	1	Student Newspaper
Spectrum	1	Student Newspaper
St. Alban News	1	Student Newspaper
State News	1	Student Newspaper
Sting	1	Student Newspaper
Stinger	1	Student Newspaper
Student Class Project Newsletters	1	Student Newspaper
Sword and Shield	1	Student Newspaper
Tattler	1	Student Newspaper
Teen to Teen	1	Other
Tejas	1	Other
Tempo	1	Student Newspaper
Terrapin	1	Yearbook
Texas Review	1	Student Alternative Press
Thing	1	Student Alternative Press
Tiger	1	Student Newspaper
Today's Aspirante	1	Student Newspaper
Tolerance Day Symposium	1	Speech
Torch	1	Yearbook
Tour de Farce	1	Student Alternative Press
Tower	1	Yearbook
Town Cryer	1	Student Newspaper
Trojan	1	Student Newspaper
Tufts Daily	1	Student Newspaper
Twisted Times	1	Student Alternative Press
University Daily	1	Student Newspaper
Valhalla	1	Student Newspaper
Vector	1	Student Newspaper
Vulcan News	1	Student Newspaper
Western Hemisphere	1	Student Newspaper
What's Bruin	1	Student Newspaper
Windup	1	Yearbook
Yates Years	1	Student Newspaper
Your Side	1	Student Newspaper

Bibliography

Attacks on the Freedom to Learn. Washington, D.C.: People for the American Way, 1981-.

Bates, Stephen. "The Textbook Wars." *The National Review*. # 45 (September 20, 1993), 65-69.

Berninghausen, David K. *The Flight from Reason: Essays on Intellectual Freedom in the Academy, the Press and the Library*. Chicago: American Library Association, 1975.

Berns, Walter. *The First Amendment and the Future of American Democracy*. New York: Basic Books, 1970.

Buckley, William F., Jr. *God and Man at Yale: The Superstitions of "Academic Freedom."* Chicago: Henry Regnery, 1951.

Burress, Lee. *Battle of the Books: Library Censorship in the Public Schools, 1950-1985*. Metuchen, N.J.: Scarecrow, 1989.

---. "A Brief report on the 1977 NCTE censorship survey," in *Dealing With Censorship*, James E. Davis, editor. Urbana, Ill.: National Council of Teachers of English, 1979, 14-47.

Busha, Charles H. *Freedom Versus Suppression and Censorship: With a Study of Attitudes of Midwestern Public Librarians and a Bibliography of Censorship*. Littleton, Colo.: Librarians Unlimited, 1972.

Censorship News. New York: National Coalition Against Censorship, 1974-.

Clor, Henry. *Obscenity and Public Morality: Censorship in a Liberal Society*. Chicago: University of Chicago Press, 1969. Reprinted 1985.

Cornog, Martha. *Libraries, Erotica and Pornography*. New York: Oryx Press, 1991.

Curry, Richard O., editor. *Freedom at Risk: Secrecy, Censorship, and Repression in the 1980s*. Philadelphia: Temple University Press, 1988.

Davis, James E., ed. *Dealing with Censorship*. New York: H.W. Wilson Co., 1979.

Demac, Donna A. *Liberty Denied: The Current Rise of Censorship in America.*
    New York: PEN American Center, 1988.

Downs, Robert B., and Ralph E. McCoy, editors. *The First Freedom Today:
    Critical Issues Relating to Censorship and to Intellectual Freedom.*
    Chicago: American Library Association, 1984.

D'Souza, Dinesh. *Illiberal Education: The Politics of Race and Sex on Campus.*
    New York: The Free Press, 1991.

Fiske, Marjorie. *Book Selection and Censorship: A Study of School and Public
    Libraries in California.* Berkeley: University of California Press, 1968.

Harris, Michael H. "State, Class, and Cultural Reproduction: Toward a Theory
    of Library Service in the United States." *Advances in Librarianship.*
    14 (1984): 211-252.

Hentoff, Nat. *Free Speech for Me But Not for Thee: How the American Left
    and Right Relentlessly Censor Each Other.* New York: HarperCollins
    Publishers, Inc., 1992.

---. *The First Freedom: The Tumultuous History of Free Speech in America.*
    New York: Delacorte Press, 1988.

Hopkins, Diane McAfee. "A Conceptual Model of Factors Influencing the
    Outcome of Challenges to Library Materials in Secondary School
    Settings." *Library Quarterly.* 63 (January 1993): 40-72.

---. "Perspectives of Secondary Library Media Specialists about Material
    Challenges." *School Library Media Quarterly.* 21 (Fall 1992): 15-24.

---. "Challenges to Materials in Secondary School Library Media Centers:
    Results of a National Study." *Journal of Youth Services in Libraries.* 4
    (Winter 1991): 131-140.

---. "Factors Influencing the Outcome of Library Media Center Challenges at
    the Secondary Level." *School Library Media Quarterly.* 18 (Summer
    1990): 229-224.

---. "Toward a Conceptual Model of Factors Influencing the Outcome of Chal-
    lenges to Library Materials in School Settings." *Library and Information
    Science Research.* 11 (July-September 1989): 247-271.

Intellectual Freedom Manual. Compiled by the Office for Intellectual Freedom
    of the American Library Association. 3rd ed. Chicago: The Association,
    1989.

Kamhi, Michelle Marder. *Limiting What Students Shall Read.* Washington,
    D.C.: Association of American Publishers, 1981. ERIC, ED 210 771.

---. *Two Treatises of Government*, edited by Peter Laslett. Cambridge: Cam-
    bridge University Press, 1989.

Locke, John. *Treatise of Civil Government and a Letter Concerning Toleration*,
    edited by Charles L. Sherman. New York: D. Appleton-Century, 1937.

McKee, Richard E. "Censorship Research: Its Strengths, Weaknesses, Uses,
    and Misuses," in *An Intellectual Freedom Primer*, Charles H. Busha,
    editor. Littleton, Colo.: Libraries Unlimited, 1977, 192-220.

Meiklejohn, Alexander. *Free Speech and Its Relation to Self-Government*. New York: Harper & Brothers, 1948.

Mill, John Stuart. *On Liberty: With the Subjection of Women and Chapters on Socialism*, edited by Stefan Collini. Cambridge: Cambridge University Press, 1989.

Milton, John. *Selected Prose*, edited by C. A. Patrides. Columbia: University of Missouri Press, 1985.

Molz, R. Kathleen. "Censorship: Current Issues in American Libraries." *Library Trends*. 39 (Summer/Fall, 1990): 18-35.

National Commission on Libraries and Information Science. *Censorship Activities in Public and Public School Libraries, 1975-1985*. A Report to the Senate Subcommittee on Appropriations for the Departments of Labor, Health and Human Services, and Education and Related Agencies. Washington, D.C.: The Commission, 1986. ERIC, ED 270 125.

Newsletter on Intellectual Freedom. Chicago, Ill.: American Library Association. 1970-.

Noble, William S. *Bookbanning in America*. Middlebury, Vt.: Paul S. Eriksson, 1990.

Oboler, Eli. *Defending Intellectual Freedom: The Library and the Censor*. Westport, Conn.: Greenwood Press, 1980.

Park, J. Charles. "Clouds on the Right: A Review of Pending Pressures Against Education," in *Dealing with Censorship*, James E. Davis, editor. Urbana, Ill.: National Council of Teachers of English, 1979, 96-107.

Pope, Michael. *Sex and the Uneducated Librarian: A Study of Librarians' Opinions on Sexually Oriented Literature*. Metuchen, N.J.: Scarecrow, 1974.

Reichman, Henry. *Censorship and Selection: Issues and Answers for Schools*. Chicago: American Library Association/ American Association of School Administrators, 1988.

Schrader, Alvin M. "A Study of Community Censorship Pressures on Canadian Public Libraries. *Canadian Library Journal*. 49 (February 1992): 29-38.

Schrader, Alvin M., Margaret Herring, and Catriona de Scoss. "The Censorship Phenomenon in College and Research Libraries: An Investigation of the Canadian Prairie Provinces, 1980-1985." *College and Research Libraries*, 50 (July 1989): 420-432.

Serebnick, Judith. "A Review of Research Related to Censorship in Libraries." *Library Research*. 1 (Summer 1979): 95-118.

Student Press Law Center Report. Washington, D.C.: Student Press Law Center, v. 1 (1974-.

Thomas, Cal. *Book Burning*. Westchester, Ill.: Crossway Books, 1983.

Ward, David V. "Philosophical Issues in censorship and Intellectual Freedom." *Library Trends*. 39 (Summer/Fall 1990) 83-91.

Woods, L. B. *A Decade of Censorship in America: The Threat to Classrooms and Libraries, 1966-1975*. Metuchen, N.J.: Scarecrow, 1979.

Woods, L. B., and Cynthia Robinson. "Censorship: Changing Reality." Paper presented at the Annual Convention of the American Library Association, Philadelphia, 1982. Washington, D.C.: ERIC, ED 226 740.

Woods, L. B., Cynthia A. Robinson, and Bernie Schlessinger *Keeping the Devil Away from Miss Jones: Censorship in Academia, 1976-1980*. Washington, D.C.: ERIC, ED 242 237.

Index

Adventures of Huckleberry Finn (Twain), 49, 91, 92, 119

Advocates of Intellectual Freedom, research category defined, 41

American Family Association, 58, 70-71

American Library Association, Office for Intellectual Freedom 20, 22, 113-115

American Society of Atheists, 63

Anecdotes, use in defending against complaints, 6-7

Anti-Defamation League, 105-106

Areopagitica. See Milton, John

Are You There God? It's Me Margaret. See Blume, Judy

Article 19, International Center on Censorship, 37

Association for Supervision and Curriculum Development, 20

Association of American Publishers, 20

Attacks on the Freedom to Learn, 22, 35; advocates, in censorship cases, 86-88; censored books 1981-1990, 49-50; censored films 1981-1990, 47; censored formats 1981-1990, 55, 57; censored formats 1981-1990, compared with past research, 95-96; censored titles 1981-1990, compared with past research, 91-94; censored textbooks 1981-1990, 50-51; censorship by institution 1981-1990, 59, 61; censorship by state and region 1981-1990, 54; censorship by state and region, as compared with past research, 97-100; censorship totals, by year 1981-1990, compared with past research, 94-95; censorship incidents, number reported in 1981-1990, 44-49; complainants 1981-1990, 63-66, 68-71; complainants, in censorship cases 1981-1990, compared with past research, 102-107; description, 113-114; format and purpose, 35-36; institutions, in censorship complaints 1981-1990, compared with past research, 100-102; outcomes of complaints 1981-1990, 81-82, 84-85; outcomes of complainants, 1981-1990, compared with past research, 110-112; reasons, in censorship complaints 1981-1990, 72-75, 77-79; reasons, in censorship complaints 1981-1990, compared with past research, 108-109; reviewed and evaluated, 115

About the Authors

JOHN B. HARER is the head of the Circulation Division of Sterling C. Evans Library at Texas A&M University and has published a number of refereed journal articles and books.

STEVEN R. HARRIS is Humanities Reference Librarian at the Middleton Library at Louisiana State University.